TERRORISM

AN INSTRUMENT OF FOREIGN POLICY

TERRORISM

AN INSTRUMENT OF FOREIGN POLICY

KSHITIJ PRABHA PH.D.

INTERNATIONAL ACADEMIC PUBLISHERS
COLORADO SPRINGS, CO
WWW.IACADEMICBOOKS.COM

International Academic Publishers Ltd.
P. O. Box 26290
Colorado Springs, CO 80918
USA

Library of Congress Cataloging-in-Publication Data

Prabha, Kshitij
    Terrorism: An Instrument of Foreign Policy /Kshitij Prabha.
    p. cm.
    Includes bibliographical references and index.
    ISBN 1-58868-076-2 (paper) -- ISBN 1-58868-077-0 (hbk.)
    1. India--Foreign Relations--Pakistan. 2. Pakistan--Foreign
    Relations--India. 3 Terrorism--India I. Title.

    DS385.5.15 P73 2000
    327.5491054--dc21

                                        00-063178

Printed in the United States of America.

Dedicated
to
my parents

Shanti Kumar & Indra Sen Kumar

Foreword

It gives me a deep sense of gratification to write the foreword to the book *Terrorism: An Instrument of Foreign Policy* authored by Dr. Kshitij Prabha. Terrorism as a manifestation of the internal frustration and alienation of sections of civil society differs fundamentally from terrorist activities sponsored by one state against another to carry out subversion, destabilization and fragmentation of the targeted state. This kind of state-sponsored terrorism is an instrument of foreign policy whose objectives should, by definition, be considered perverse and as posing a profound threat to the stability, integrity and unity of the states involved.

At the global level, cross-border terrorism sponsored by individual states poses a threat to international peace and development. The September 11, 2001 attacks on the World Trade Center (WTC) in New York and the Pentagon in Washington D.C. and the retaliatory bombardment of Afghanistan by the U.S. has brought this concern to the attention of the international community.

Terrorism of different kinds has been a feature of international politics since the beginning of recorded history, but it assumed more potent and dangerous content and dimensions since the end of World War II. The speed in communication, more dangerous arms available for terrorist purposes, their free availability on the international arms market, have all combined to make terrorism a lethal instrument of subversive politics.

A compounding factor increasing the critical fallout of terrorism is the linkage between various terrorist groups and the governments that sponsor and support them. These linkages contribute to the intensity of terrorist acts across national frontiers. They also provide logistical, financial, weapons and organizational support to terrorist groups.

While the U.S. is only now feeling the impact of international terrorism, India has faced the challenge of externally sponsored terrorism and subversion right from the time of its emergence as an independent country. Terrorists and separatists elements operating in

India have at different points of time received support from China, Pakistan Bangladesh, and Myanmar. Jammu and Kashmir, Punjab and the northeast states of India, as well as Tamil Nadu, have been subjected to terrorist activities originating in foreign countries or being supported by external elements. India has faced insurgencies for nearly five decades now, some of which were encouraged as instrumentalities of foreign policies of other countries. Apart from several hundred common citizens losing their lives, India has lost two Prime Ministers, one Chief of Army Staff and several senior public figures and government officials, due to terrorism.

The increase in terrorist attacks against India, sponsored by Pakistan, after the Kargil conflict in 1999, and the more recent high-jacking of the Indian Airlines flight from Kathmandu to Delhi, are the latest examples of terrorism being utilized by Pakistan as an instrumentality of its foreign policy objectives, vis-à-vis India. It is in this context that I consider this book by Dr. Kshitij Prabha, not only timely but a very relevant contribution to the study of the dangerous and destabilizing phenomenon of terrorism. Her six chapters cover the conceptual, the factual, and operational dimensions and ramifications of terrorism comprehensively. Her analysis has a depth and range which makes it a uniquely structured study of problems arising out of terrorism.

This is a study which would be useful both for scholars and decision makers. Chapters 2, 3 and 4 of the book, dealing with the conceptual aspects of terrorism in Punjab, are of particular relevance to our current predicaments. The sub-section dealing with terrorism as an ultimate instrument of Pakistani foreign policy in chapter 5, also merits focused attention. Dr. Kshitij Prabha has made not only a necessary but a commendable contribution to the study of the problems related to terrorism by writing this book. It deserves to be studied not only by all those interested and concerned about the ramifications of the problem, but it is my view that the book will constitute a long-term source of reference to future students dealing the with issue.

J.N. DIXIT
Former Foreign Secretary, and
Member National Security Advisory Board
Government of India

Contents

Preface

Terrorism is one of the controversial issues that has threatened political stability and territorial integrity of nation-states. The September 11, attacks on the World Trade Center (WTC) in New York and the Pentagon in Washington D.C. and the resulting military action by the U.S. against Afghanistan show just how terrorism has far reaching implications for global peace and regional security. Though an abundance of literature is available on terrorism, yet few substantial studies leading towards an understanding its conceptual aspects and its impact on international relations have been published.

While common people suffer from the spectre of terrorism, scholars are busy debating whether to consider terrorism an end in itself or a means to an end. Both the terrorists and the states sponsoring terrorism take advantage of the gap in understanding the subject. Thus terrorism continues to threaten civilized society.

Terrorism, particularly when sponsored by a nation-state, has certain characteristics that need to be analyzed for better understanding. This is critical because terrorism abetted by a group can be contained; but if sponsored by a state, it is difficult to curb without influencing the foreign policy of other nations. This aspect of terrorism has raised alarm all over the world, and foreign policies of many nations are being reviewed to cope up with this reality in international relations. It seems more and more nation-states are ready to use terror tactics to achieve their foreign policy objectives. This needs to be examined before the whole world gets affected by this new trend in international politics.

The present study is an effort towards the same. The conceptual examination of terrorism is followed by an analysis of impact on foreign policy with special reference to Pakistan-sponsored terrorism in India. I hope it provides insights into the problem of terrorism in international relations and helps all peace-loving nations to counter-act this tragic phenomenon.

New Delhi   KSHITIJ PRABHA

Chapter 1

Introduction

The study of terrorism as an instrument of foreign policy will remain abstract if not based on a clear understanding of the concept of foreign policy. A perceptive insight into foreign policy is a prerequisite to understanding the meaning and relevance of terrorism in international relations. Therefore, this study begins with a brief description of foreign policy. Since terrorism is hypothetically considered as an instrument of foreign policy, other instruments of foreign policy are also discussed briefly at the very onset.

Every nation has certain objectives to achieve in international relations. Once a nation-state comes into existence, it becomes part of the global political system. It is difficult for a nation to maintain its socio-economic and political growth in isolation. The existing world order is such that all nations are dependent on one another to serve their national interests. This implies that every nation has some objectives to achieve. A government, therefore, deliberates its foreign interests and adopts some as objectives. These resolutions become the guiding principle in the decision-making process the outcome of which is described as foreign policy in the dictionary of international politics.[1]

The making of foreign policy depends on various issues such as external threat, geographical location, strategic significance, political aspirations, economic requirements, ideology, personality of the statesmen and overall national interests of the country. Significant among these is national ethos or ideology of a nation and the national interest. Notwithstanding the fact that realism is key to successful implementation of foreign policy, ideology too plays an important role. As a matter of fact, it is one of the dominant factors in foreign policy making of many Islamic states and all those inclined towards maintaining religious identity. Islamic states are classic examples of countries adopting ideology in foreign policy making.

However, the national interest factor is also vital to every nation, be it motivated by religionism or political modernism. Scholars all over the world agree to the relevance of national interest in foreign policy making.[2] A nation adopts policy that jives with the national interest and safeguards its ideology, history and economic requirements. In brief, foreign policy decisions are made in response to events and problems that have already occurred in the past, are anticipated in future,[3] and their prospective implications on national interests of the country. Thus foreign policy-making could adversely effect the politico-economic agenda of the nation. Therefore, it is subject to special consideration and serious examination before arriving at any position.

The policy of a government that has direct or indirect bearing on the global political system; and through which a nation plans to achieve goals across its borders is known as foreign policy. It is important to note that while focusing on national interest, foreign policy also takes the international situation into consideration. The question about whether to prioritize national interests over global concerns has been debated time and again. The bottom line remains that foreign policy is often influenced by both domestic and international conditions.[4] This is especially relevant to the politico-economic conditions of the developing countries which rely on economically advanced nations for infrastructure and technology. They cannot ignore their socio-economic conditions which demand foreign aid and assistance; and simultaneously have to consider its implications on international politics. It is worth mentioning that there are certain policies which are not foreign policy as such but have a far reaching impact on international politics. For instance, the government of South Africa adopted apartheid, a policy of racial discrimination, for implementation within the territorial boundaries of the country. But it affected the international community to such an extent that the UN imposed economic sanctions against South Africa compelling the government to change the policy.[5] Obviously, foreign policy cannot be separated from domestic policy in an absolute sense. Theoretically, however, foreign policies are meant for external implications.

FOREIGN POLICY INSTRUMENTS IN INTERNATIONAL RELATIONS

Foreign policy dominates international relations. Its importance should be understood in the light of the fact that it is the only policy that proposes interaction among nations and thereby determines global politics.

Foreign policies are normally manifested in bi- and multilateral agreements. These agreements could be of various kinds— political, military, cultural, economic and so on. The most significant amongst them all, however, are military alliances which affect international politics to a great extent. The North Atlantic Treaty Organization (NATO) could be taken as an example of such an agreement at the multilateral level where more than two nations are involved in collective policy making. On the other hand, bilateral agreements represent policies of two countries. These agreements, be they bilateral or multilateral, have direct implications on the foreign policy of nation-states which decides the course of international politics.

At the very onset it needs to be reiterated that foreign policy is not an end in itself but a means to achieve goals of nation-states in international relations. In pursuit of the realization of foreign policy objectives a nation employs the following instruments:

1. Diplomacy
2. Propaganda
3. International Law
4. International Organizations
5. Foreign Aid
6. Overt Warfare

These are acceptable means in achieve foreign policy goals. Nation-states have used these instruments from time immemorial. War and diplomacy are amongst the ancient instrumentalities, whereas others have evolved over more recent times. Since the focus of the present study is terrorism as an instrument of foreign policy, a detailed account of the above-mentioned instruments is not relevant of this time.

FAILURE TO ACHIEVE FOREIGN POLICY GOALS THROUGH CONVENTIONAL INSTRUMENTS

Diplomacy, propaganda, international law, international organizations and overt warfare are conventional and acceptable instruments through which foreign policy goals can be achieved. Humankind discovered these instruments during the evolution of the nation-states as political units. And as the nation-state came into being, the need for interaction among different nation-states became inevitable. Thus in the due course of time all these instruments of foreign policy became acceptable.

The evolution of new instruments per se is a manifestation of inherent weaknesses in the existing instruments of foreign policy. War, the oldest of all, was the most prevalent instrument during the primitive era, prior to what may be called the "social contract" era of the evolution of societies. With the emergence of states the idea of diplomacy and negotiation came into existence. During this period overt war became less significant and was substituted by new instruments. It needs to be emphasized that when one instrument loses its significance in international relations, a new instrument in tested for better results. In this process, numerous instruments are created to accommodate requirements of the nations concerned. The Arab-Israeli conflict bears testimony to this fact. In an attempt to resolve the conflict between the two, each and every conventional instrument has been employed from time to time. Not a single conventional instrument of foreign policy is left untried to bring the two to agreement. War, diplomacy, propaganda, international law and international organization all are used to try to defuse tensions between the two. Three wars—1948, 1966 and 1973—were fought between Israel and Arab states; conferences and dialogues were held at the diplomatic level at Camp David and in Geneva. Similarly, economic and defense assistance was provided by the superpowers in favor of one or the other.

In 1948, the UN took the responsibility to resolve issues and formulate principles for the creation of two of separate states in the disputed territory, the outcome of which was the UN resolution on Palestine. Similarly, both parties disseminated propaganda to influence world opinion. Unconventional and unethical means, such as deception and violence, have also been used to achieve to try to solve the problem. However, all these efforts have failed to bring rapprochement between the two. Most of the year 2001 was marked by intense violence between Israelis and Palestinians.

An important issue on in the matter of failure to achieve foreign policy goals through conventional means is to achieve the causes of failure i.e. why a government fails to achieve goals through conventional means. This could be analyzed from two perspectives which are shown in Model I.

Model I
Causes for Failure to Achieve Foreign Policy Goals through Conventional Means

	Ambiguity of Approach (1)	Hostility (2)
1. Diplomacy	Which form of diplomacy to employ	Non Compromising Stand
2. Propaganda	Self-Contradictory	False Propagation
3. International Law	Interpretation	Disobedience
4. International Organization	Obscure Genesis	Disobedience
5. War	Objective of War	With equal power status

From the perspective of the ambiguous approach it could be argued that, diplomacy fails to achieve foreign policy goals of a nation because of its ambiguous application. For instance, during the early phase of hostility between India and China, diplomacy through negotiation and conferences did not work whereas Ping Pong or Table Tennis "diplomacy" opened the door for negotiation and friendship during the late 1970s. India made efforts to normalize relations between the two countries through negotiation and dialogue, but could not achieve a breakthrough until China sent the table-tennis team to play with India as a good will gesture. It was the beginning of understanding between India and China. Soon after, India sent a delegation to participate in the Canton Trade Fair. China welcomed this move and subsequently a trade agreement was signed between the two as the process towards normalization of relations.[6]

George Fernandes' often quoted remark that China is the number one enemy of India also reflects upon the ambiguous approach in so far as India's foreign policy towards China is concerned. On one hand, the Government of India intends to normalize relations with China, on the other hand, the defense minister scruples the process by expressing such statement. This could lead towards failure in achieving India's foreign policy goal in China.

The second important factor is hostility between nation-states which leads to non-compromising attitudes. The example of India's diplomatic effort to resolve the Kashmir tangle with Pakistan during the early 1950s could be taken as a case. India was initially keen to negotiate with Pakistan on territorial claims in Jammu and Kashmir, but then later adopted a non-compromising stand. The Pakistani Government refused to withdraw from Pakistan occupied Kashmir (PoK) and hence all the diplomatic efforts to conduct a plebiscite, as agreed upon at the UN, failed.

Similarly, propaganda fails to realize foreign policy of a nation because of its self-contradictory nature and false propagation. For instance, Pakistan's propaganda about human rights violations in Jammu and Kashmir which, even if true, would be mainly because of terrorism caused by Pakistan's involvement, contradicts its allegations against India. In other words, on one hand, the government of Pakistan creates an environment in which the violation of human rights is more likely to occur, on the other hand, it accuses India of the same. Thus, it gets trapped in its own false propaganda and fails to achieve its objectives. Propaganda devoid of facts bears no fruit. It has to be supported by certain factual evidence, without which it loses credibility. The same situation prevailed in 1948 when Pakistan accused India of aggression at the Geneva Convention of the International Committee of the Red Cross (ICRS).[7] Pakistan used propaganda against India, but failed to influence world opinion mainly because there was no truth to the allegations.

In the context of international law as an instrument of foreign policy, failure results from either ambiguity of interpretation or disobedience. Law as such is subject to interpretation, more so international law, because of its pluralistic nature. International law has often been interpreted to suit the foreign policy of individual nation-states and is also often defied.

The veto power of the five permanent members of the UN Security Council could be cited as an example. These members veto any resolution adopted by the UN if it does not suit their foreign policy interests. Vetoed issues remain inconclusive and at times are withdrawn from the agenda. These issues are normally left to be settled at the bilateral level discussions. The case of Azerbaijan in 1946 was the first matter of this kind that came before the Security Council. The Soviet Union vetoed all the efforts of the Council and ultimately the issue was left to direct negotiation between the contenders. The dispute on the status of Jammu and Kashmir between India and Pakistan also met the same fate. These are some of the examples were international law has been defied. This failure is mainly because of multiple interpretations of International Law.

Likewise, international organizations too fail to achieve foreign policy objectives of a nation. First, because their very foundations are laid in an environment of insecurity and second, because different nations have different objectives to achieve irrespective of the principles laid down by international organizations. In some cases the principles laid down themselves are ambiguous. For example, the Nonaligned Movement (NAM) rejected the idea of alignment with either the Eastern or Western military blocs, but in the 1970s welcomed some countries affiliated to these military blocs. Many countries joined the NAM forum without any commitment to the ideology of neutrality which was the turning point in the history of NAM. It was after this phase that gradually NAM lost its significance in international politics. It is worth mentioning that once an international organization fails to hold to its principles, member nations tend to disassociate from that particular body. This is another important reason for the failure of international organizations.

Finally, war fails to achieve goals of foreign policy of a nation because of ambiguity in the objectives of war. For instance, in the 1971 war, Pakistan fought on the issue of Bangladesh and hence the open confrontation should have remained confined to India's eastern front only. But instead, Pakistani armed forces launched attacks in Jammu and Kashmir as well.[8] The outcome was a lack of proper concentration and a humiliating defeat for Pakistan in East Bengal.

Similarly, the objective of the U.S. in the Gulf War was not merely the liberation of Kuwait, but also to oust Saddam Hussein from power and to destroy chemical weapons plants. In fact, Iraq's armed intervention in Kuwait served as an opportunity for the U.S. to attack Iraq. Though the Iraqi forces withdrew from Kuwait, the U.S. failed to topple Saddam from the saddle of power because multiple objectives dominated the decision. The U.S. attacked Iraq as the savior of Kuwait rather than as the destroyer of Saddam.

Another reason for the failure of war to achieve foreign policy goals of a nation is confrontation with an equally powerful nation. War can achieve the purpose only if fought with a relatively weaker state. The Korean war, which practically was war between two superpowers, could not be fought to an end in favor of either of the two, the U.S.-led South Korea and the Soviet-led North Korea. But the contenders, the U.S. and the former Soviet Union, fought to retain the entire Korea under the influence of either the U.S.-led liberal democracy or the Soviet-led Communism. But neither of the two could win the war. Ultimately, Korea was divided into two North and South —under the influence of the former Soviet Union and the U.S. respectively. They failed to retain the entire country under their domain because it was war between two equally strong and powerful nations.

Obviously, various instruments have been employed by nation-states from time to time to achieve their foreign policy goals in international relations. It is explicit that these instruments are not foolproof and are largely dependent on the international environment. There are many variables in relations among nations that can determine the failure or success of these instruments.

Hitherto, I have examined the application and failure of foreign policy instruments acceptable to international society. But there are other means which in spite of being practiced, are not included in the list of foreign policy instruments available to nation-states. Terrorism is one among these.

Maintaining progression in the evolution of ideas in international relations, the present study highlights the emergence of this "new" instrument for the realization of foreign policy goals of nation-states. This study based on an in-depth analysis of Pakistan's use of terrorism in two states of the Indian Union – Punjab and Jammu and Kashmir illuminates the strengths and weaknesses of this instrument in achieving foreign policy goals.

TERRORISM AS AN INSTRUMENT OF FOREIGN POLICY
In international politics a stage comes when conventional instruments of foreign policy fail to influence international relations and conflict becomes inevitable. But if the situation is

not so blatant as to justify overt warfare or the international environment is not conducive to conventional war, terrorism becomes a viable alternative.

In brief, terrorism could be analyzed as a symbolic act designed to influence political behavior by illegal means.[9] While conventional instruments of foreign policy are used to maintain diplomatic relations among nations and influence their policies in a normal situation, terrorism encompasses only one aspect—to influence policy of a nation in an unfriendly environment. Being an unconventional instrument, terrorism can be employed in a positive way to maintain diplomatic relations. On the contrary, it aims to destabilize an established government by means of violence and conspiracy, and it is this specific nature of terrorism that makes it a threat to the international body politic.[10] Application of terrorism to achieve foreign policy goals has become a serious concern compared to other instruments, because while on one hand, it is often used by some nation-states, on the other hand, virtually all nation-states deny their involvement. To put it precisely, it is an undeclared means to achieve foreign policy objectives.

Use of terrorism in international relations goes back to political developments in the Middle East after the creation of Israel in 1948, and the refusal by Palestine leaders to accept the UN proposal for two separate states in the disputed territory. While Israel came into being as an independent sovereign state, Palestine remained deprived of her territorial rights. This was the beginning of the growth of terrorism in the Middle East. Ever since then, the foreign policy of Israel has been prone to the use of counter terrorist tactics in dealing with the Palestinians who adopted a violent path to the liberation of their homeland. Israel made it clear by, its actions, that terrorism by the PLO would not be tolerated, and that the agencies or nations co-operating with them would also be punished. Thus, nations involved in the Israel-PLO conflict also resorted to terror tactics such as killing, sabotage, kidnapping, hijacking, arson etc. Syria's involvement in sponsoring terrorism against Israel is an example of this phenomenon. Over time, the entire Middle East has become the most active zone of terrorism. Toward the end of 2001, as this book was going to press, Israel was again engaged in anti-terrorist military operations in PLO-controlled territories following a number of suicide attacks that left many Israelis dead. The peace process was at a standstill.

Another landmark in the history of terrorism is the case of Libya under the leadership of Col. Qaddafi. The Libyan government headed by the Revolutionary Command Council from 1969 and under the leadership of Qaddafi has been committed to a radical ideology and aggressive foreign policy which has spread as far as Europe and America besides the Middle East. Qaddafi formed a mercenary force called the 'Islamic Legion' and set up guerrilla training camps in Libya to support the liberation movement in Northern Ireland,[11] and thus sponsored terrorism as far as Europe and America.

The U.S. too, has not lagged behind in the use of terrorism to accomplish its foreign policy goals. While in the Middle East, the U.S. adopted a policy of counter-terrorism, in South American countries the story was different. The U.S. has utilized every opportunity and instrument—not excluding what some would see as terrorism—to influence or to impose its policy on neighboring South America, be it to contain expansion of Soviet Communism or to combat the illegal drugs industry.

It is interesting to note that the disintegration of the Soviet Union and subsequent end of the Cold War gave the impression that international terrorism would come to an end, but this is far from practical reality.

While it is true that the collapse of the Soviet Union eliminated the rivalry between Moscow and Washington and left the U.S. the sole world power, the absence of a rival and equally strong superpower in the international political system has created a dangerous vacuum. Nations are trying to adjust to the new world order. While Germany and China are vying to replace the Soviet position, the regional powers have lost the umbrella of superpower protection and are groping in the jungle of the new world order. They are exploring ways and means to achieve their foreign policy goals at the regional and bilateral level. A sense of insecurity prevails upon and among the central and south Asian countries, especially those used as puppets by superpowers during the Cold War era.

The best example of escalation of terrorism in the post-Cold War situation was the use of Afghan Mujahideens by Pakistan to achieve its foreign policy goals in Jammu and Kashmir. The stockpile of arms and ammunition left behind by the U.S. and the Soviets were conveniently available to Mujahideens. Pakistani leaders are keen to bring the Muslim dominated countries of this region into an Islamic block and thereby influence regional politics of Central Asia. The common boundary of Afghanistan with the new Muslim Central Asian Republics (CAR) like Tajikistan and Uzbekistan makes it strategic for Pakistan its in pursuit of the realization of this goal. The fact that Pakistan appears to be siding with the U.S. in the aftermath of the September 11, 2001, attacks does not necessarily mean it has abandoned this goal. It may well be that Pakistan saw the U.S. intervention as an opportunity not only to get more military aid from America but also a chance to control the future politics of Afghanistan.

Thus, instead of a recession, we should actually anticipate an escalation of terrorism in south and central Asia. Therefore, it is high time that the phenomenon of terrorism was thoroughly examined and its conceptual aspects understood without any prejudice. It needs to be analyzed as it exists, and not as it suits our interests. Terrorism has emerged as a concept in the realm of political science in the same way that other theories and 'isms' have evolved in the history of political thought.

REFERENCES

1. For detailed discussion on foreign policy see Hans J. Morgenthou and Kenneth W. Thompson, *Principles and the Problems of International Politics* (New York: Alfred A. Knopf, 1950); Joseph Frankel, *The Making of Foreign Policy* (New York: Oxford university Press, 1967); James Rosenou, *Domestic Sources of Foreign Policy* (New York: The Free Press, 1967); Richard C. Snyder et al., Others, *Foreign Policy Decision Making* (New York: The Free press, 1962).

2. Hans J. Morgenthou, *Politics Among Nations* (New York: Alfred A. Knopf, 1950), p.21 also see, James Rosenau, *Domestic Sources in World Politics* (New Jersey Englewood Cliffs, 1958), pp. 2-4.

3. John P. Lovell, *Foreign Policy in Perspective* (New York: Rinehart Winston, Inc., 1970), p. 208.

4. P.M. Kamath, *Foreign Policy Making and International Politics* (New Delhi: Radiant Publishers, 1990), p. 68.

5. *African Recorder: A Fortnightly Record of African Events*, 15th-28th January, 1992, (New Delhi), p. 8753.

6. *Date India*, 20, 16th-22nd May, 1977 (New Delhi: Press Institute of India, 1977).p.307.

7. *Indian Express* (Bombay), 31st August, 1993, p. 7.

8. K.P. Candeth, *The Western Front: Indo-Pak War 1971* (New Delhi:

12 · Terrorism: An Instrument of Foreign Policy
Allied Publishers, 1984), p. 37.

9. Paul Wilkinson, *Political Terrorism* (London: Macmillan Press, 1974), p. 18.

10. Stephen Segaller, *Invisible Armies* (London: Michael Joseph, 1986), pp. 10-20.

11. Admiral Stansfield Turner, *Terrorism and Democracy* (Boston: Houghton Miffin Co., 1991), p. 217, also Aftab Kamal Pasha, Libya and the U.S.: Qaddafi's Response to Reagan's Challenge (New Delhi: Détente Publications, 1984), pp. 1-11.

Chapter 2

Conceptual Aspects of Terrorism

WHAT IS TERRORISM?

The word terrorism is understood by scholars in different ways. There are innumerable definitions of terrorism and every definition appears correct in its own light. However, if these definitions were analyzed in their totality, perhaps an acceptable definition would evolve. It is because of multiple interpretations that the meaning of political terrorism has not been understood in the correct manner and its application is defended, be it by individuals, groups of individuals or an established sovereign nation. As a matter of fact, terrorists continue to threaten humankind because there is no commonly agreed definition of the term; hence no agreement on appropriate punitive action to be taken against the perpetrator is possible either by the state or international organizations.

Scholars all over the world are entangled in the labyrinth of terminology and have expressed different views. Amongst them all, the most widely acceptable definition is the one given by Yonah Alexander. He defines terrorism as: "The use or threat of violence against random or civilian targets in order to intimidate or to create generalized pervasive fear for the purpose of achieving political goals."[1]

Somewhat similar is the elaborate definition given by Alex P. Schmid who analyzed innumerable definitions before concluding that

> Terrorism is an anxiety-inspiring method of repeated violent action, employed by clandestine individual group or state actors, for idiosyncratic, criminal or political reasons,

whereby—in contrast to assassination—the direct targets of violence are not the main targets. The immediate human targets of violence are generally chosen randomly or selectively from a target population, and serve as message generators. Threats and violence based communication processes between terrorists, victims, and main targets are used to manipulate the main target, turning it into a target of terror, a target of demands, or a target of attention, depending on whether intimidation, coercion or propaganda is primarily sought.[2]

This definition goes into detail about the phenomenon of terrorism. But it remains more focused on targets and objectives rather than its basic nature.

Similarly, Brian Jenkins writes that the threat of violence, individual acts of violence or a campaign of violence designed primarily to instill fear is terrorism.[3]

This definition of terrorism is very close to the idea of terrorism, but lacks two significant aspects, i.e. training and international support. These two aspects are highlighted in the definitions given by Christopher Dobson and Martha Crenshaw. The necessity of training is expressed by Dobson who writes that "use of explosive devices used by terrorists needs appropriate training."[4] The need for international support is expressed in the definition given by Martha Crenshaw, who explains that "terrorism is a means to accomplish certain political objectives with international support."[5]

There is yet another group of scholars who define terrorism from a historical perspective. For instance, Michael Walzer believes that random terror for political achievement emerged as a strategy of revolutionary struggles after World War II.[6]

Likewise, one group of scholars defines terrorism as violence and repression used by the government or the state itself. For example, Walter Laquer writes that "acts of violence and repression as carried out by governments against their own people is terrorism."[7] In the same tune Neil Livingston opines that the state is the main perpetrator of terrorism today.[8] Corroborating the same idea, scholars like Jay Mallin define terrorism as a substitute for overt warfare. To put it in his words, "When diplomats fail soldiers take over, when soldiers fail terrorists take over,"[9] which actually is far from the practical reality. As a matter of fact, when diplomats, politicians and police fail soldiers take over to curb terrorism.

United Nations Definition of Terrorism

The spectre of terrorism dominated international politics too such an extent that in 1972, the UN General Assembly adopted a resolution to establish an Ad Hoc Committee to take "measures to prevent international terrorism which endangers or takes innocent human lives or jeopardizes fundamental freedoms, and study of the underlying causes of those forms of terrorism and acts of violence which lie in misery, frustration, grievance and despair, and which cause some people to sacrifice human lives including their own, in an attempt to effect radical changes." In line with this resolution the Ad Hoc committee created three sub-committees. The first of these was dedicated to examining the definition of terrorism. Seven draft proposals were submitted by member nations. The Nonaligned Group defined terrorism as acts of violence committed by a group of individuals, which endanger human lives and jeopardize fundamental freedoms the effects of which are not confined to one state. The NAM draft proposal, however, excluded the inalienable right to self-determination under colonial and racist regimes from this definition. The French proposal defined terrorism as heinous acts of barbarism committed in foreign territory. Similarly, the Greeks defined terrorism as criminal acts of violence … with the aim to achieve some objective. Haiti highlighted the political purpose of terrorism. Iran, Venezuela and Nigeria added the flavor of freedom fighting into the definition. The multidimensional proposals apparently ended in deadlock in so far as the definition of terrorism was concerned. The matter remained suspended until 1987 when the UN Secretary General convened an international conference to define terrorism and differentiate it from freedom fighting. And finally the member nations agreed to define all acts of terrorism as "criminal."

Can we describe terrorism as criminal? If analyzed conceptually terrorism cannot be defined as criminal. The link between crime and terrorism could be established, but to identify the two as one would be misleading. However, if it is analyzed for administrative purpose, the UN definition perhaps is the simplest way to counter international terrorism. If prevention is the objective of defining terrorism as criminal, then the UN should have simultaneously adopted a resolution on compulsory extradition among member nations. Unless extradition is made compulsory and terrorists (criminals) are tried according to the law of the nation they belong to, this definition too has no relevance.

It is obvious that there is a long list of definitions offered by scholars as well as by international organizations. However, as mentioned at the very onset all these definitions have certain common factors, which could be collectively analyzed to evolve a working definition of terrorism. This definition is presented here as a model (Model II).

Model II
Definition Model of Terrorism (Based on David Easton's Systems Theory)

TERRORISM

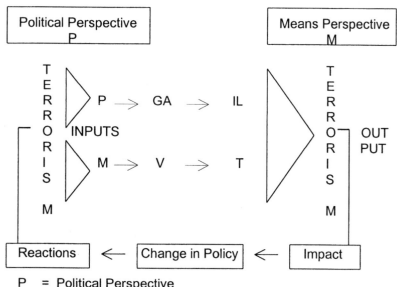

P = Political Perspective
GA = Group Action
IL = International Linkages
M = Means
V = Violence
T = Training

In this model, the definition of terrorism is described in two broader perspectives – Politics (P), i.e. terrorism as a political phenomenon, and Means (M), i.e. to study terrorism as means to achieve certain political objectives and not an end by itself. In the subsequent phase, the model explains that P helps actors to form a cohesive whole, which subsequently results into Group

Actions (GA), and GA leads to International Linkage (IL). From the point of the political perspective, terrorism is defined as a political rather than criminal or psychological phenomenon, as it aims to achieve political power and not accumulation of wealth or personal gain. In the Means (M) perspective, terrorism is defined as a means to achieve political objectives rather than an end. The model goes further to explain that the means employed is violence (V) and the violence employed is also of specific type, i.e. tactical which needs professional training. A layman cannot operate sophisticated weapons used by terrorists. This aspect also has to be incorporated in the definition of terrorism. A detailed explanation of both the perspectives is given in Model II.

Terrorism as a Political Phenomenon
Violence and intimidation could be used for any purpose. It could be used for individual gain and also for economic and social problems. But as a game of politics, only those acts of violence and intimidation could be defined as terrorism which aim to accomplish political objectives. Violence and coercion employed by individuals for personal gain is more of a psychological nature than political. Socio-economic or psychological aspects are causal factors in the growth of terrorism but not the basic nature of the phenomenon. The nature of terrorism is political and so is its objective. Its political identity could be analyzed by various elements involved in terrorism such as objective, methods, and the organizational structure. The objective of a terrorist group is invariably political such as autonomy or secession to acquire political power. Social and economic issues are not primary to them. They believe that once the political power comes in to their hands, social and economic reforms would follow by themselves. Thus to acquire political power is their sole aim,[10] not economic prosperity. Their target of violence is also related to politics as they aim to kill political leaders and destroy political institutions to malign the credibility of the government concerned.

Furthermore, terrorists are organized as a political party. Terrorist groups come into being as a political unit aspiring for certain political ideology. When they fail to achieve their political goal by political means, in due course of time, their priority shifts from active politics to tactical violence. Take for instance, the case of the All India Sikh Students Federation (AISSF). The AISSF came into existence as an organized group of Sikh students. But with the passage of time, it emerged as the most active terrorist group in Punjab. When such organizations fail to gain favor from the government and the people, they adopt violence to destabilize the government[11] and create mass unrest and fear in a democratic society, wherein every faction of society, including the militants, enjoy freedom of thought and action. It is because of these aspects that Wilkinson defines such acts of violence as political terrorism.[12]

Subsequently, the definition model highlights GA as an essential element of political terrorism. The kind of violence that terrorists employ cannot influence a society without collective effort of a group in which one member depends on the other to achieve the goal. Their actions are inter-dependent without which conspiracy and sabotage cannot work. The need for cooperation within terrorist groups is so high that, terrorists have to depend upon members from other organizations sometimes beyond their national boundary.[13] For example, in order to instill pervasive fear and violence, Inter Services Intelligence (ISI) the CIA of Pakistan, takes assistance from different terrorist groups active in Punjab, Jammu and Kashmir and Assam. Their acts of terror are examples of GA rather than an individual effort.

Individual terrorists are psychopaths and are generally novices in the art and craft of violence nor do they have any political purpose. For example, the man who shot Pope John Paul II in Rome had no political motives. The convict Mohamed Ali Agea of Turkey was inspired by his personal convictions. The Italian investigation agencies tried to establish a link with "Grey Wolf"—a terrorist group based in Turkey,[14] but could not get any evidence of his political connection. He was put on trial and sentenced to death. Throughout the trial he denied having any connection either with "Grey Wolf" or the right wing Nationalist Action Party (NAP) in Turkey. On the contrary, he claimed to be representing a new form of terror of his own. Such individual acts could be identified as psychological cases, a kind of mental sickness or a sort of professional criminal employing violence and intimidation to accumulate wealth for personal gain or name without any political purpose.

The political perspective on terrorism would remain incomplete if international links were not analyzed. Interaction among members of terrorist groups is an essential feature of terrorism. It is difficult for terrorists to operate within national boundaries where their activities are under the constant vigil of police and intelligence departments. Besides, terrorism involves heavy expenditure on arms, ammunition and training to run the organization. This requires huge amounts of money that are unlikely to come from sources within the country. If exposed, they would be subjected to punishment and torture by law enforcement agencies. Therefore, most of the terrorist groups rely on assistance from across the borders.

The history of terrorism is replete with examples of transnational terrorism. The Red Faction Army (RAF) of the former West Germany, popularly known as Baader Meinhof, and Jammu and Kashmir Liberation Front (JKLF) could threaten governments concerned because of their international linkage. Baader and Meinhof, the two important leaders of RAF had rendezvous in Jordan to train Palestinian militants[15] and received support in the mission to destabilize the government of West Germany. In the same way Kashmiri militants receive military and financial assistance from Pakistan, Afghanistan and from NRI in Canada and the U.S. Similarly, besides the U.K., the IRA has branches in America.[16] The former British Prime Minister Margaret Thatcher claimed to have authentic information that the IRA was receiving funds from Libyan mercenaries. This was one of the important factors that made Thatcher approve of U.S. attacks on Libya in 1986.[17] Without such contacts and assistance terrorism cannot challenge an established system.

Terrorism as a Means to an End
The second essential aspect in the definition of terrorism is to analyze it as a means to an end rather than an end by itself. History is evident that terrorism—even when it involves suicide attacks—invariably aims to achieve certain socio-economic or political goals.

Terrorism has never been an end but a means to an end.[18] Even in cases of individual terrorism, there is always certain social or economic objectives to achieve. Individual terrorist carry grievances against the system, which is expressed in violent form. Martha Crenshaw substantiated this idea when she clearly defined terrorism as a means to a political end.[19] And it is the type of means employed, i.e. tactical violence that describes a group as terrorist or otherwise. It is worth mentioning that in pursuit of their political goals, terrorists do not employ political means. They, instead, adopt violence and criminal paths to accomplish their goals. Notwithstanding the fact that, in the beginning, terrorist groups operate as a political party, at the later phase they switch over to violence and intimidation when the concerned government rejects their demands.

It needs to be emphasized that political parties too resort to violence at times. A clear distinction between violence perpetrated by a political party and a terrorist group is necessary because in the definition of terrorism, there is always a tendency to identify both as one and the same, whereas there are differences between the two. For instance, violence by a political party is haphazard and of low intensity. It takes place only in the wake of protest rallies and demonstrations. These are more in the form of anomie than planned violence like that of terrorism. Violence by political parties does not create mass unrest, though it does create temporary chaos in administration.

Terrorism, on the other hand, adopts a well-planned tactic to indulge in violence, arson and subversion. Every phase of violence is planned by terrorists according to the socio-economic and political conditions of the target area. An environment of unrest and fear is created through conspiracy and propaganda before terrorists resort to violence.

As a corollary to this and as explained in the model, it is also important to mention that violence, being a pre-condition of terrorism, needs planning for implementation which largely depends on training imparted to the terrorists. Without proper training in the use of arms, violence cannot achieve its purpose. Thus, training camps are set up to train members of terrorist groups. They are trained in use of weapons, telecommunications and post-violence follow up actions. Imparting training to terrorists is a necessity because the era we live in is not that of daggers and knives, but of machine guns, bazookas, missiles, transistor bombs, letter bombs, chemical weapons, and, as we saw in the U.S. on September 11, 2001, passenger planes being used as weapons of destruction. These are highly sophisticated weapons and operations that require proper training.[20]

Apparently, terrorism is not just an expression of political violence that takes place at the spur of the moment, but an organized instrument to achieve political objectives. It has its own identity, comprising of various elements as mentioned earlier. Therefore, terrorism could be defined as an act or threat of an act of tactical violence by a group of trained individuals, having international linkage, to achieve political objectives. These groups could be either sponsored by state or non-state agencies. The sponsorship doesn't change the basic nature of terrorism. It remains the same. This definition of terrorism is precise and covers all the aspects of terrorism.

ARE TERRORISTS FREEDOM FIGHTERS?

Defining terrorism is difficult because it raises controversy. There is one group of political scientists who believe that terrorists are freedom fighters. To them one man's terrorist could be another's freedom fighter.[21] Such contentions complicate the definition of terrorism.[22]

Calling a terrorist a freedom fighter and vice versa is an extreme example of the dilemma. Terrorism has its own identity and so has freedom fighting. U.S. Senator, Henry Jackson expelled the idea of identifying the two as one and the same in the following words: "It is a disgrace that democracies should allow the treasured word 'freedom' to be associated with acts of terrorism."[23]

What is true is the fact that terrorists are misguided members of society who aim to destabilize an established system and risk their own lives. This is why scholars like Michael Arson believe that terrorists are cruel members of society not freedom fighters.[24]

While on one hand, scholars play the game of terminology, on the other hand, rebel and frustrated groups of society continue to threaten humankind by adopting terrorism as a means to achieve political goals. It is, therefore, important to draw lines between a terrorist and a freedom fighter. Though the issue is too controversial to be accepted without criticism, it does not mean that differences cannot be explained. The difference between the two are analyzed in the light of the following determinants:

Relevance of the UN
Objective and Means to an Objective
Nature of Violence
Colonialism and Decolonisation
Lack of Moral Justification
National Versus International

Relevance of the United Nations

Though scholars have interpreted terrorism from different perspectives, they have not explored the relevance of the UN in curbing terrorism.

The UN is the only international body where nations have committed themselves to collective security. The member nations have entrusted the UN with the responsibility to maintain the global political system in a peaceful manner. It has been empowered to recognize a nation, i.e. whether a particular nation is to be given recognition as an independent state or as a province within a nation. Notwithstanding the fact that the UN has no right to dismember or to carve out a new state, it is expected that its offices could be utilized to resolve such international disputes, particularly those that cause threats to international peace and security. One good recent example of this phenomenon is the independence of Namibia, which was occupied by South Africa. It become an independent sovereign nation in the late 1980s after the general election conducted under the auspices of the UN. The most recent is the case of East Timor in Indonesia where people voted for independence under the supervision of the UN.

The significance of the UN[25] could be analyzed in the light of the fact that once a nation is recognized under the UN charter, no individual or group of individuals of that particular country could be recognized as freedom fighters, as this would promote sub-nationalism within a country and could promote disharmony, civil strife, and ultimately anarchy could prevail. Freedom fighting or the right to self-determination is well recognized by the UN as an inalienable right of the people. It does not, however, mean that some of the genuine cases of freedom fighting, one like that of India or Israel prior to their independence would be allowed as the guiding force for secessionist movements in a country which is already liberated from the foreign yoke. It needs to be emphasized that so long as an individual or a group of individuals hold the nationality of an independent sovereign nation, as recognized by the UN, they have no moral or legal right to claim themselves as freedom fighters. Their acts of violence should be identified as acts of terrorism rather than freedom fighting.

Objective and Means to an Objective

The second distinction between the two is in the objectives. The main objective of freedom fighters is to acquire independence by any available means, be it moral or immoral, legal or illegal, whereas the primary objective of a terrorist is violence and intimidation. What they claim to be their political or economic objective are not "objective" as such but "a set of demands". An objective is a well-perceived plan, while demands are simply expressions of the desires of an individual or group of individuals. Neither policy nor any plan of action is required to press a demand, as the demand itself is a part of a certain objective. It needs to be mentioned that in their pursuit to achieve independence, freedom fighters submit a list of demands some of which are accepted by the government concerned. However, irrespective of acceptance or rejection, freedom fighters do not deviate from their main purpose, i.e. to achieve independence. The same cannot be said of terrorists. There is evidence of recession in the level of violence and terror when the government accepts terrorists' demands. For instance, the leaders of the Naga and Mizo rebellions during the 1960s in India abandoned their violent course of action as soon as the governments of India accepted their demands.

Apparently, demands rather than objectives motivate terrorists. This is precisely because objectives of terrorist groups are deceptive and ambiguous. They are deceptive in the sense that their ulterior goal is secession, but they compromise on partial autonomy or release of their colleagues. As a matter of fact, terrorists resort to violence and terror to get their demands accepted rather than to achieve any broader objective. On the other hand, freedom fighters are motivated by the objective and to achieve that, unlike terrorists, they sacrifice trivial demands.

Independence is the goal of freedom fighters. But terrorists do not have determined objectives and even if they claim to have some,[26] they are deceptive and fluctuating. They ultimately tend to become victims of self-deception and puppets of their own illusions and disillusions. It is rightly said that terrorism as an objective is a failure.[27] This is precisely because there is a gap in understanding amongst members of terrorist groups. The PLO and IRA had internal dissension because of conflicting opinions. The IRA was divided after the civil rights movements in Northern Ireland because rival leaders disagreed on how to respond to the demands of the Catholic population.[28] Similarly, the PLO was split on the issue of how to defeat Israel. Not only are they divided on the question of methodology but also on their objectives. At one phase they claim to be fighting for independence, at the other, they are satisfied with partial autonomy. The same is not true of freedom fighters. Their objective is well defined and there is no deviation from it. There are innumerable examples of terrorists renouncing the violent course of action, but there is no example of surrender in the history of freedom fighting.

Nature of Violence

The third significant difference between the two is related to magnitude of violence. Terrorists are known for violence that creates fear psychosis.[29] This is such an important aspect of terrorism that scholars like Brian Jenkins define terrorism in terms of violence and intimidation. He opines that the threat of violence, individual acts of violence, or a campaign of violence designed primarily to instill fear, is terrorism[30]

On the contrary, violence is not a pre-condition for freedom fighting. It is only under repressive foreign regimes that freedom fighters too resort to violence. In other words, it could be said that the magnitude of violence in cases of freedom fighting shifts frequently according to prevailing situations. Their solitary aim is liberation at any cost and by any means, through peaceful negotiation or tactical violence. Violence is not an essential condition for freedom fighting. Freedom could be achieved through peaceful means too. For instance, the non-violent path adopted by Mahatma Gandhi for the independence of India was acknowledged far and wide. He was very much a freedom fighter and under no circumstances was he ever declared a terrorist by the British government.

Violence, however, is all in all for terrorism. Philosophy and utility of violence influence the very concept of terrorism. There can be no terrorism without violence. It is a must and the only means adopted by terrorists. The same is not true with freedom fighting. Violence used by a freedom fighter is aimed at government agencies rather than innocent people. Targeting innocent lives is typical of acts of terrorism whereas freedom fighters try to protect them. Thus, on the basis of uses, magnitude and nature of violence also a terrorist act could be seen differently from that of a freedom fighter.

Colonialism and Decolonisation

To call a freedom fighter a terrorist is the brain child of colonialism. After the renaissance and industrial revolution in Europe, western countries marched towards colonialisation of Afro-Asian countries. After having conquered them, the colonial powers adopted repressive policies to exploit rich mineral resources of these countries. When natives realized the economic intentions of the ruling foreign powers, they organized themselves as resistance forces and indulged in violence and terrorist activities. These people were branded as terrorists by the colonial governments; and when colonialism was at the apex and extremist organizations were gaining mass support the ball went into the native's court. They justified their violence as part of the struggle for freedom from the foreign yoke. Frantz Fanon made it clear that "violence alone, violence committed by the people, violence organized and educated by its leaders make it possible for the masses to understand social truth and gives the key to them. Without that knowledge of practice of action there is nothing but a fancy dress parade and blare of the trumpets."[31] Extremists were influenced by his philosophy.

The era of colonialism, however, has passed. The Afro-Asian countries, which were under colonial power, are now independent sovereign nations except for a few pockets here and there. It is ironical that the den of terrorism is not small fragmented colonies, but those Middle East, South Asian and Latin American countries that have achieved independence from the foreign yoke.

The point of our concern is: can we justify freedom fighting in a country that has already achieved independence from foreign power? If terrorism prevails upon India, Pakistan or Sri Lanka and terrorists call themselves freedom fighters, what could be the justification?

In a country, which has achieved independence after a long relentless effort, there could be no moral or legal justification. It would rather undermine the concept of sovereign states. To consider a terrorist as a freedom fighter in a liberated democratic country would mean political destabilization. In every nook and corner and for any trifle cause, people could organize themselves as freedom fighters bringing about a precarious state of affairs, specifically in a pluralistic society. This would promote sub-nationalism[32] and political chaos. Terrorists are not freedom fighters but murderers.[33] Even in cases of human rights violation or issues of right to self-determination, terrorism should not be encouraged as freedom fighting. The issues involved in the struggle for freedom are negotiable and could be resolved more efficiently through negotiation than by violence, which is, counter productive. A country gets involved in a vicious circle of violence and counter-violence when terrorism comes to exist causing irreparable damage to mankind.

Lack of Moral Justification

As mentioned, freedom fighters too resort to violence for independence, i.e. to liberate people from foreign exploitation. Their objective is to secure civil and political rights for the masses by any available means. It is because of this commitment that freedom fighters are honored as heroes and their acts of violence are morally justified.[34] Whereas terrorism is considered immoral, selfish and criminal because unlike freedom fighting their objective is not liberation but intimidation and killing.

The basic principle of terrorism hinges around rejection of civilized society. For this reason alone acts of terrorism lack moral justification. Their acts of violence create panic in the socio-political environment of a society. The same is not applicable in so far as freedom fighting is concerned. Their target of violence is not crowded placed like markets, malls, railway stations or business offices where common people become victims. A freedom fighter takes special care that innocent masses are not trapped in their violence. They purposely avoid targeting such locations because killing innocent by-standers, shoppers or people at work is immoral. Freedom fighters generally try to achieve the goal without deviating from moral course of actions, though they do get caught in the dilemma of end and means. But the same is not true with terrorism. Terrorism aims to create fear psychosis to achieve its goals. As a result, no morality justifies terrorism. But all ethical values support the movement for the independence of a country.

National Versus International

Another significant difference between a freedom fighter and a terrorist is related to the scope and area of influence. Freedom fighters limit their activities to the national boundaries of their country. Their means and end are confined to geographical boundaries. They do get moral support from foreign countries, but are not dependent on them. Their target as well as modus operandi is limited, that keeps them constantly in touch with the people. It would be difficult for freedom fighters to achieve their goal without the cooperation of the masses, as an independence movement is aimed to liberate people from the bond of slavery; and without their support independence would remain a far cry to achieve.

Unlike this, terrorism is transnational by its very nature. Notwithstanding the fact that terrorism also aims to achieve certain political objectives, it does not rely on the means available to terrorists from within the region. It seeks assistance from across the border and uses international forums to get their demands accepted. They operate in an interwoven organizational structure, which is spread all over the world. They recruit members from the international community to perpetrate violence and terror in any part of the world. Crossing international borders to maintain new contacts and to acquire arms is the routine job of a terrorist organization. Apparently these acts are transnational by nature.

The foregoing discussion makes it obvious that there is hardly any similarity between a terrorist and a freedom fighter except for the fact that freedom fighters too use violence at times. The same is not applicable to terrorism. Violence is all there is for terrorists. The most significant difference between a terrorist and a freedom fighter, however, is related to the relevance of the UN because except for this all the arguments for and against could be justified. But once the UN Charter consciously accepts a nation, its citizens ought not be treated as freedom fighters. If this delineation is not maintained, terrorism will continue to threaten civilized society.

TERRORISM AND INSURGENCY

Another important problem with the definition of terrorism is related to terrorism and insurgency. These two are often treated as one and the same. Thus in this section a detailed distinction between the two is presented.

The *Encyclopedia of Social Sciences* defines insurgency as use of armed forces against an established government to achieve a public purpose which cannot, in the opinion of the insurgents, be achieved by pacific means.[35] It is also defined as struggle between a non-ruling and ruling body in which the former consciously employs political resources and violence to establish legitimacy for certain issues considered as illegitimate.[36] Though the political system is the main target of insurgents, their motivating factors are rooted in social and economic disparities. It is true that both terrorism and insurgency can be means for violent revolutionary change. But there are differences between the two, which could be analyzed by following Model III.

Model III
Pattern of Violent Revolutionary Change

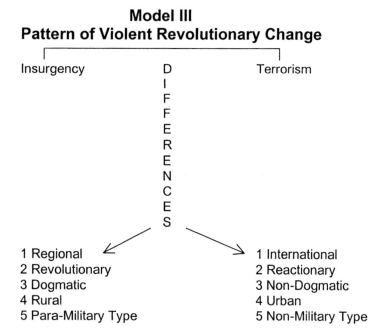

Insurgency	D	Terrorism
	I	
	F	
	F	
	E	
	R	
	E	
	N	
	C	
	E	
	S	

1 Regional	1 International
2 Revolutionary	2 Reactionary
3 Dogmatic	3 Non-Dogmatic
4 Rural	4 Urban
5 Para-Military Type	5 Non-Military Type

Regional and International

The first dividing line between insurgency and terrorism is the fact that, while the former is regional the latter is international by nature. Insurgency remains confined within the nation or within its neighborhood. The experiences of France in Algeria and the U.S. in Vietnam were manifestations of this phenomenon. Andrew M. Scott went to the extent of describing the need of appropriate physical and demographic environment as an essential condition for successful application of insurgency.[37] Insurgency needs access to territory and sanctuary which is safe from army attacks and close to the border of a nation sympathetic to the rebels. For instance, Americans despite being armed with sophisticated weapons, could not succeed in Vietnam because of lack of local support. But the same is not applicable to terrorism. Violence inflicted by terrorists knows no boundary, while insurgency remains confined to a specific state. Though there are cases of insurgency funded by foreign lands, it is worth noting that their actions seldom affect the international community. The same cannot be said for terrorism. It is perpetrated far and wide all over the world and this phenomenon concerns the international community. Terrorism does not remain confined to one region nor do members belong to any one region, community or race. Terrorist groups recruit people from different parts of the country, as their targets are world wide whereas insurgency involves local people. Their recruitment is based on commitment to the cause and geographical knowledge of the region, which is not the case in so far as terrorism is concerned.

Revolutionary and Reactionary

The second important difference between the two is in their character. While terrorism is reactionary, insurgency is revolutionary in character.

Terrorism is an expression of a reaction in response to social, political and economic conditions. It is not a planned movement but reaction to a certain situation, which according to the terrorists, is injustice and cannot be tolerated, whereas insurgency is well planned and every phase of the struggle is chalked out as to suit their objective. Violence perpetrated by insurgents is not a reaction to any situation but a planned movement to achieve their goal, i.e. revolution. In other words, insurgency is aimed at revolutionary change while in the case of terrorism the objective remains obscure. They put forward certain demands, which if accepted by the government terrorism recedes and if not, it could be bargained. In brief, there is always scope for compromise in terrorism, but insurgency stays committed to its ideology and goal.

Dogmatic and Non-dogmatic

The third aspect of the distinction between insurgency and terrorism is related to ideology, i.e. while insurgency is dogmatic, terrorism is non-dogmatic.

The concept of revolution goes back to the Greek city-state when Aristotle for the first time did a thorough and systematic study of revolution. But the idea of revolution or revolutionary change did not influence the political process (except for the American and the French Revolution which took place in 1773 and

1789 respectively) until Marx's theory of revolution gained momentum. As a matter of fact, revolution by insurgency drew the attention of political scientists with the rise of Communism in Southeast Asia, Latin America and Africa. In this context, Brian Crozier has rightly observed that major post-war insurrections in Southeast Asia were inspired by Communism.[38] Similarly, Abdul Haris Nasution, the Indonesian commander who fought against the Dutch between 1945 and 1949, emphasized that the ideological fight is usually the strongest motivation for insurgency and guerrilla warfare.[39]

These are some of the characteristics with which terrorism has nothing in common. Unlike this, terrorism is non-dogmatic. The objective, besides being obscure, is not supported by any fixed ideology. Their demands and objectives as mentioned earlier, keep shifting from one to another as per the response they receive from the government and the people. This flickering tendency is because they lack ideology. The causes of terrorism are rooted in socio-economic and political deprivation, but there is no fixed ideology to motivate them for their cause. This is why terrorists employ hit and run tactics rather than a systematic method to achieve their ambiguous objectives.

Rural and Urban
The fourth significant difference between insurgency and terrorism is related to geographical location. By virtue of being revolutionary in nature, insurgency depends on rural support for its struggle. Its roots are in the countryside because it aims to liberate common men from certain bondage. Therefore, the support and confidence of the masses is vital to their cause, and second, because the seat of administration is invariably located in urban areas, it helps insurgents escape from the marauding eyes of law enforcement agencies. This in turn, helps insurgents to mobilize rural masses and the infrastructure available to them. If people were convinced that the cause they were fighting for is genuine, they would extend their cooperation without which insurgency would fail. Simultaneously, by operating in rural areas, insurgents can defeat counter actions by the government. The geographical conditions like bushes, mountains, valleys and jungles are conducive to requirements of insurgents. They find rural surroundings more suitable and prefer to use country made

weapons than sophisticated weapons from abroad.

Terrorism, on the contrary, is based in urban society. The Tupamaros of Uruguay, the Weather Underground of the U.S. and the IRA have all focused their activities in sophisticated and densely populated cities. Urban life is prone to criminal activities. Its socio-economic conditions nurture conflict and dissidence.[40] The wide gap between the rich and the poor, unprecedented sufferings, mental agony, tensions and access to sophisticated weapons create an environment where the individual becomes inclined to violence to achieve his objectives. Those at the bottom of the socio-economic hierarchy in the urban society tend to become professional terrorists to make quick bucks. The sophisticated infrastructure and communication facilities available to the city life make terrorists mobile and successful in their hit-and-run tactics. It is not a coincidence, therefore, that the September 11, 2001, attacks on the U.S. were masterminded in major cities of the U.S., U.K. and Germany.

Para-Military and Non-Military Type

Finally, differences between insurgency and terrorism could be also analyzed in the light of organizational structures of terrorist groups. Guerrilla or insurgent groups are organized on military lines.[41] They believe in blind obedience to the command in the same way as regular armed forces demand. The guerrilla insurgency advances as per the instruction of the commanding authority. Their targets are the armed forces of the government and its agencies in the vicinity. Insurgents operate collectively and do not propagate individual heroism. Their organization and modus operandi is more like a paramilitary organization rather than a terrorist group. Insurgents are conscious of the fact that guerrilla tactics cannot defeat a well-established army of a nation without mass support. A favorable public opinion thus becomes an important prerequisite for the success of their venture.

Unlike this, terrorism is unorganized, and believes in kidnapping and killing innocent masses. Insurgents do not create terror by killing innocents, whereas terrorists bank upon indiscriminate violence and killing. They are neither trained like the regular army nor well organized. The history of terrorism is replete with individual charisma of Guevera, Meinhof, Marighella and so on. The same is not applicable to insurgency. Command is not as important an issue in terrorism as in insurgency. Subversion and killing have to go on be it haphazard or in order. The mode of operation is immaterial in terrorist operations. The goal has to be achieved. Whether an individual or a group carries out an operation, is not relevant. Therefore, on the basis of the modus operandi too, terrorism and insurgency could be evaluated separately. The problem in separating the two is mainly because both belong to the same school of political thought that practices violence. However, to consider them as one is to commit a conceptual error, as they are totally distinct phenomena.

ECONOMIC AND POLITICAL CAUSES OF TERRORISM

Having discussed the differences between terrorism, freedom fighting and insurgency, it is appropriate to analyze causes of terrorism without which the conceptual study of terrorism would remain incomplete. This section highlights economic and political conditions as the main causes of the rise of terrorism.

There are various causes of terrorism, such as psychological, social, economic, and political. But one element, i.e. frustration is common to all rebels.[42] Frustration generates anxiety; anxiety causes loss of metal equilibrium; and at the bottom of frustration lies the socio-economic conditions. Some scholars define this phenomenon as maladjustment in the socio-economic and political system.[43]

Innumerable adjustments are made in politics to serve the interests of a group. These adjustments clash with the interests of other groups. For instance, because of special favor accorded to one group, other groups remain deprived of the privileges enjoyed by the former. Scholars describe this practice of maladjustment in different ways. Karl Marx defined it in the light of capitalism versus socialism; while Hadley Centril considers it as domination over freedom.[44] These are important factors for the rise of terrorism. Whether analyzed from capitalist, Marxist or humanist interpretation, the fact remains that economic deprivation and social injustice is the main cause for the growth of terrorism. Such conditions leave indelible marks in the personality make up of an individual as well as that of the society. The following section analyses these economic and political factors.

Economic Factors

The economy plays a significant role in the growth of terrorism. It is through economic resources that essentials of life—food, clothes and shelter—come from. If human beings are deprived of basic necessities, a sense of insecurity, anguish and frustration prevails. Often such psychological conditions cause violence and terrorism.

Terrorists believe that they are rightfully entitled to have all the essentials and comforts that they are deprived of but others are enjoying.[45] They consciously reject the fact that economic equality has never existed in the history of humankind. Inequality is the natural way of life and people are aware of this social condition. However, social awakening under the influence of Marx's theory of communism got people swayed and some began to believe that the wide economic disparity that exists in society is the handiwork of a few rather than a natural phenomenon that could be accepted as a normal living condition. This awareness brought a new desire to overcome economic deprivation by force and violence. This intense desire is also fueled by the exhibition of wealth by the higher classes in the society.[46] The economic resources and infrastructure available, yet inaccessible, agitate the minds of the deprived class.

The same theory could be applied in international relations as well. There is a wide gap between rich and poor countries. They often confront each other on various economic and political issues.[47] The developing countries are deprived of advanced infrastructure facilities and are dependent on the developed nations for the same. It is difficult for poor developing countries to bargain with the rich countries. Reverse financial flow and debt crisis are important issues because developing countries find themselves dependent and hence cannot exercise their free will in global issues of their concern.

International terrorism is also one of the areas where weaker nations are unable to influence policies of other states. For instance, in spite of being committed to the cause of Palestine, the Arab nations could not persuade Israel and the U.S. to an early settlement of the dispute. To a great extent, this is precisely because the Arab countries are dependent on the U.S. and the West for production and marketing of oil and petroleum products. It would have been difficult for the Arab nations to receive advance technology essential for the growth of infrastructure had they applied pressure tactics to resolve the Palestine-Israel dispute. The support given to the U.S. by some Arab nations in the Gulf War and more recently, in the war in Afghanistan may also be attributed to this fact.

In addition, there is the possibility that regional differences among nations might lead to political violence by people in the less privileged regions.[48] Scholars like Willy Brandt have warned that "often war is thought of in terms of military conflict, but there is an equal danger from mass anger caused by economic disaster."[49]

Political Factors

Political issues have equally contributed to the growth of terrorism. This dimension should be understood in the light of the fact that once basic economic needs are fulfilled, desires for power and position dominate human psychology. Terrorism, being one of the means to acquire power, is also inspired by the same psychodynamics of humankind. The obscure purpose of terrorism is to acquire power through secession, autonomy or revolution.

Politicization of violence is the tactic terrorists use to gain public support.[50] Unless they make a case for a greater common cause, such as liberation, autonomy, secession and so on, terrorism is unlikely to receive public attention without which the very purpose of terrorism would be defeated. The objective of terrorist groups is not only to create fear psychosis but also to prove that terrorism is a viable instrument in politics.[51]

A brief note on tactics of terrorism would help us understand political aspects of terrorism. The first tactic employed by terrorists is to obtain political recognition for their cause. In the pretext of fighting for a common cause, they justify their violent course of action. They want to change existing political systems by means of violence, intimidation, kidnapping, killing, hijacking, bombing and subversion.

The political nature of terrorism could also be traced in various forms of violence adopted by terrorists. While it is a matter of fact that they kill innocent masses, the truth is that their targets are political leaders, who live in high security zones. Since political leaders are not easily accessible, they kill innocent people. But the fact remains that their ultimate targets are political leaders, ministers, heads of state, diplomats and other important personalities.[52] This is precisely because publicity is vital in terrorism. By killing politicians and diplomats, they gain more political mileage than by killing innocent shoppers or travelers.

Another important tactic of terrorism is propaganda, which is an important element in the realm of politics. Terrorism needs an audience, and propaganda is an easy mode of communication available to terrorists. They propagate a philosophy of violence and accordingly influence public opinion through media especially in a democratic system. Take for example, how Osama Bin Laden's speech, released soon after the U.S. launched its retaliatory attacks on Afghanistan, was carried by all major broadcasting services in the U.S. and all over the world. It could be argued that the world's most wanted terrorist was given a chance to further propagate the message of violence.

To conclude the discussion on causes of terrorism, it needs to be reiterated that growth of terrorism is not merely because of economic and political deprivations, but also because of social disparity, psychological depression, lack of creativity and misinterpretation of different religious codes. At the same time, it is also important to note that, except for the religious and psychological factors, all other aspects are not significant to this study and thus left to be analyzed in separate works on sociological aspects of terrorism.

TERRORISM AS A TRANSNATIONAL PHENOMENON

Another relevant aspect in this conceptual analysis of terrorism is its international linkage. Terrorism as a concept is a global phenomenon. This aspect also needs to be highlighted in the conceptual study of terrorism. Terrorism is an international phenomenon, be it employed by revolutionary groups or sovereign states. The phenomenon, which came into existence as sordid means to acquire wealth and power, has gradually emerged as one of the instruments to achieve political goals by revolutionary groups and rogue states.

Terrorism, either sponsored by a group of by an independent state, cannot challenge an established political system without foreign assistance. This phenomenon is also described as transnational terrorism. The international linkage of terrorism is highlighted in the following paragraphs.

Acts of political violence and intimidation that transcend an established geo-political boundary and go beyond acceptable norms of international law and diplomacy, are known as international terrorism. Such acts of violence are carried out by both autonomous non-state actors at the behest of a state involved in abetting terrorism or by the state itself. Libya, Syria, Iran, Israel, Pakistan, Cuba, the U.S. and many more could be included as examples of states using terrorism to achieve their foreign policy goals.[53] The very fact that terrorism is used to realize foreign policy goals, makes it obvious that terrorism has far reaching implications on international relations. Several nations expressed their concern about this phenomenon but nothing substantial was done to curb the growth of international terrorism, in spite of all the resolutions adopted by the UN, until the attacks on the U.S. on September 11, 2001.

However, long before this incident, it was well known that terrorist groups, sponsored by states, operate in a huge web-like organization, which has an international network. Terrorism is transnational by nature in the sense that it involves individuals of different nationalities in the operations and influences the political processes of many countries. In other words, it is the externalization of internal warfare deliberately defying national borders.[54] All the characteristics of transnationalism defined by scholars as contact, coalitions and interactions across state boundaries, that cannot be controlled by the central foreign policy organs of government, have found manifestation in the concept of modern terrorism.[55]

But, as U.S. investigations on the September 11 attack show, it is not merely border crossing that makes terrorism an international phenomenon. The organization of the terrorist group and other related aspects such as decentralized structure, sources of financial assistance and supply of weapons and ammunition, interaction of members from one country to another irrespective of their nationality, training and targets; all collectively contribute towards making terrorism an international phenomenon. Edward Mickolus' definition of terrorism testifies to the same. He explains that terrorism is intended to influence attitudes and behavior of a target group wider than the immediate activities, and through the nationality or foreign ties of perpetrators, its location or the mechanics of its resolution, its ramifications transcend national boundaries.[56] In order to have a proper understanding of the transnational nature of terrorism, it needs to be analyzed

thoroughly, as follows, under four categories. These are:
Decentralized structure of the organization
Financial sources and supply of arms and ammunition
Interactions of members
Training and targeting

Decentralized Structure of the Organization

The first characteristic that makes terrorism an international phenomenon is its organization. The organizational structure of terrorist groups is highly decentralized and diffused. It neither consists of one unit nor functions under the command of a single individual responsible for carrying out acts of terrorism. No member of a terrorist group enjoys absolute sovereignty. The powers are shared among various units but not necessarily under a single banner or command. For instance, terrorists associated to the cause of Palestine fought under the umbrella of the PLO, but many groups existed within the broad-based organization. At times, division of powers is so strong that some acts of terrorism are condemned by the members within the same group.

The powers are delegated from one division to another for subversive activities through various smaller units spread all over the world. The JKLF, Khalistan Commando Force (KCF), Badder Meinhof and many other terrorist groups, including Osama Bin Laden's organization, operate in diffused structures. For instance, the JKLF and the KCF are fighting for the cause of Jammu and Kashmir and Punjab respectively, but their units operate in Great Britain and the U.S. as well. The assassination of an Indian diplomat at Birmingham in England by the JKLF is an obvious example of terrorist outfits and the active role they play in exerting pressure on major political issues across the world.

Similarly, on January 8, 1971, a bomb exploded in the Soviet Cultural Office in Washington D.C.[57] The Jewish Defense League (JDL) was responsible for this violence and the objective was to restrict Soviet assistance to the Palestinian militants. These are some of the examples that bear testimony to the fact that organizational structures of terrorist groups are based on the principle of decentralization, which provides wide scope for international linkage.

Financial Sources and Supply of Arms and Ammunition

The most challenging task before a terrorist group is raising funds and accessing weapons. Because of vulnerability, it is difficult to collect funds and weapons from within the national boundary. The target or the victim government is likely to identify the assisting agencies through intelligence and other sources and ban the funding sources. Therefore, the best possible source for funding lies across the border.

The terrorist groups are inspired by so called long-term goals. They avoid risks involved in seeking assistance from within the national boundary. The only solution to their problem is financial assistance from nations hostile to the target country. For instance, the best choice for the JKLF and Sikh militant groups is assistance from Pakistan. Many such groups have been funded, armed and trained by nations such as the Soviet Union, the U.S., People's Republic of China, Cuba, North Korea, Libya, Syria, Lebanon and others. To a great extent these countries have funded and supplied arms to many terrorist groups affiliated to different causes.[58]

It is worth mentioning that foreign assistance comes from both official and unofficial channels. Of the two, indirect monetary assistance through private agencies is more in practice, precisely because direct involvement in subversion goes against international law and morality. An individual nation, specifically members of the UN, cannot take the risk of being dismembered. In spite of these realities, states like Pakistan openly fund and supply arms to terrorists. While cash comes from indirect channels, the flow of weapons from Pakistan to terrorists in India is an open secret. Any individual, be it a terrorist or a common person from the street, can buy weapons at a low price from the open arms bazaar in Dara Alam Kher near Peshawar in Pakistan. As cited earlier, several nations are involved in this trade. Pakistan is not an exclusive case. In order to protect the narco-economy, Columbia, Bolivia and many others encourage terrorism across the border with the help of one another. Drug syndicates, spread all over the world, manage their nefarious business.

Interactions of Members

The third significant aspect that makes terrorism an international phenomenon is interactions among terrorists. Nationality is not an important criterion for membership in a terrorist group. Solidarity is more relevant to terrorism than national identity. Commitment to the cause beyond national boundaries promises more publicity and ensures safe operation. A terrorist involved in planting bombs at one place could be seen across the border the next day flying off to yet another far off nation with whom the victim country does not have an extradition treaty.

Though terrorists refrain from participation in issues impertinent to their national or regional aspiration, some groups do opt for active participation in international issues. For instance, Palestine's revolutionary war against Israel became a global problem. Some of the terrorists associated with the Palestine crises were Japanese nationals. By recruiting terrorists from different parts of the world, they established a global network. The most remarkable illustration of this kind of participation is the Lod Airport incident. On May 31, 1972, three Japanese gunmen attacked passengers at Israel's Lod Airport with machine guns and hand grenades killing twenty-five and injuring seventy-six. These terrorists were members of the United Red Army of Japan and were recruited by the Popular Front for the Liberation of Palestine (PFLP).[59] However, it was not an exclusive case of international participation in acts of terrorism. Different groups operating in South Asia, Central Asia, Europe, and South America also operate in global networks. The members of these groups don't belong to any particular country. They represent different parts of the world.

Training and Targeting
Finally, another significant aspect that reflects upon the transnational character of terrorism is training, camping and targeting. The scientific and technological advancement of modern weapons demands special skill therefore proper training is a must. Unless the members concerned undergo good training, it is not possible to operate weapons and implement the in action plan.

Terrorists, whether from Kashmir or Japan are dependent on foreign territory for training, because the risk factor is high within the national boundary. Camping within the nation would not be a viable proposition as law enforcement agencies can trace their whereabouts, which might put terrorists behind bars. Similarly, official training institutes and academies like that of police or armed forces cannot impart terrorist training to individuals whose aim is to destabilize governments. Armed forces are to protect and not to destabilize an established system. It is ironic that some countries are involved in imparting training to mercenary forces in order to destabilize a hostile government across the border. Such training activities are normally provided in clandestine operations because they go against international law. Thus, the only alternative left for terrorists is to set up camps beyond the national boundary with the aid and assistance of foreign agencies. This is an established fact in so far as terrorism in Jammu and Kashmir is concerned. Shabir Shah, a Kashmir terrorist who belonged to the Secessionist People's League revealed in his interview that training camps were set up with the permission of General Zia-ul-Haque in Pakistan and Pak occupied Kashmir (PoK). [60] Late in 2001, the U.S. was dropping bombs on what were believed to be terrorist training camps in Afghanistan.

Furthermore, their target is not merely the public property of a hostile nation but also its leaders, officials, diplomats and the countries friendly to them. They get involved in multiple activities all over the world and because of interdependence among the nations; almost every country is concerned about these dastardly acts. The UN would not have spent its precious time adopting resolutions on terrorism had it not been a global problem. It got involved because of its international implications. The member nations passed several resolutions beginning from 1972 to 2001, which, per se, gives extraterritorial dimensions to the problem of terrorism. Since terrorism is recognized as a transnational phenomenon, it could be logically deducted that the foreign policy of nation-states has to be affected by this new "ism" in international politics. Hence, the following chapter of the book highlights different aspects of terrorism in foreign policy decision-making.

REFERENCES

1. Yonah Alexander, *International Terrorism: National, Regional and Global Perspectives* (New York: Praeger Publisher, 1976); *Journal of International Affairs*, p. CIV.
2. Alex Schmid and J. Albert Jongman, *Political Terrorism* (New Brunswick: Transaction Books, 1988) p. 28.
3. Brian Jenkins, "International Terrorism: Trends and Potentialities", *Journal and International Affairs*, Vol. 32, No. 1, Spring/Summer, 1978, pp. 115-123.
4. Christopher Dobson and Ronald Payne, *The Weapons of Terror*, (London: Macmillan Press, 1979), p. 67.
5. Martha Crenshaw, "Theories of Terrorism", *The Journal of Strategic Studies*, Vol. 10, No. 4 (December 1987), p. 13.

6. Michael Walzer, *Political Principles* (New York: Basic Books Inc. 1980), pp. 201-203.
7. Walter Lacquer, *The Age of Terror* (London: Wiedenfield and Nilcolson, 1987), passim.
8. Neil Livingston, *The War Against Terrorism* (Massachusetts: D.C. Health and Co. 1982), p.11.
9. Jay Mallin, "Terrorism as a Military Weapon", *Air University Review*, Vol.XXVIII, No.2 (Jan/Feb 1977), pp. 54-64.
10. Lester A Sobel, *Political Terrorism*, Vol.2, (New York : Facts on File, 1978), pp. 2-3.
11. Paul Wilkinson, *Terrorism and Liberal State* (London: Macmillan Press Ltd., 1977), Passim.
12. Paul Wilkinson, *Political Terrorism* (New York: John Wiley and Sons, 1974).
13. Christopher Dobson and Ronald Payye, *Weapons of Terror* (London: Macmillan Press, 1979), p. 63.
14. Sadhan Mukherjee, *Terrorism and Antonov Case* (Delhi: Navyug Press, 1985), pp. 13-18.
15. Donna M. Sehlagheck, International Terrorism: An Introduction to Concepts and Actors (Massachusetts: D.C. Healths Co., 1988), p. 61.
16. Raymond R. Corrado, "Ethnic and Student Terorism in Western Europe", in Michael Stohl, *The Politics of Terrorism* (New York: Marcel Dekker Inc., 1979), p. 198.
17. David Carlton and Carlo Shaerif, *International Terrorism and World Security* (London: Croom Helm, 1974), p.38.
18. Martha Crenshaw, "Theories of Terrorism: Instrumental Organisational Approach", *Journal of Strategic Studies*, op.cit., p.13.
19. Christopher Dobson and Ronald Payne, *Weapons of Terror*, op.cit., p. 67.
20. Jenny Teichman, "How to define Terrorism", *Philosophy: The Journal of the Royal Institute of Philosophy*, Vol.64, No.250, (October, 1989), p.511.
21. Patric Clawson, "Terrorism in decline, "*Orbis*, Vol.52, No.2, (Spring 1988), p. 273.
22. Henry Jackson, "Terrorist and Freedom Fighters", *The Reference Shelf*, Vol.58, No.3, (New York: H.W. Wilson Comp. 1986).
23. Michael Aaronson, "Terrorism or Freedom Fighting", *International Relations*, Vol.8, No.6, (November, 1986) p. 619.
24. Paul Johnson, "The Age of Terrorism, "*New Statesman*, (London), 88, 1974, p.763.
25. A terrorist group normally aims to achieve autonomy or creation of a separate state, which does not come easily unless based on certain valid ground. Their object remain for fetched; and thus they shift towards violence and intimidation as their goal, which does not draw attention of masses, an essential condition for liberation movement.
26. Martha Crenshaw, "Theories of Terrorism", *Journal of Strategic Studies*, op.cit., pp.13,15.
27. J. Bowyer, Bell, *The Secret Army: A History of IRA* (Cambridge: MIT,

1974).
28. Richard E. Rubenstein, *Alchemists of Revolution* (New York: Basic Books, 1987), p.198.
29. Brian M. Jenkins, *New Modes of Conflict* (Santa Monica: Rand Corporation, 35th Year), p.a., 90406.
30. Frantz Fanon, *Wretched of Earth* (London: Penguin Books, 1965), p. 118.
31. D.M. Sehlagheck, *International Terrorism*, op.cit., pp. 31-45.
32. Michael Aaronson, :Terrorism or Freedom Fighting", *International Relations*, Vol.8, No.6, (London), 1986, p. 619.
33. D.J.C. Carmichael, "Of Beasts, God and Civilised Men: The Justification of Terrorism and Counter-Terrorist Measures", *Terrorism: An International Journal*, Vol.6, No.1, (New York, 1982).
34. Frederick Schuman, *Encyclopedia of Social Sciences*, Vol7, (New York: MacMillan & Co., 1932), p.117.
35. Bard E. O'Neil et al., *Insurgency in the Modern World* (Colorado: West View Press, 1980), p.1.
36. Andrew M. Scott and Others, Insurgency (Carolina: University of North Carolina Press, 1970), p.8.
37. Brian Crozier, *The Rebels* (London: Chetto and Windus, 1960), pp. 37-45.
38. Abdul Haris Nsution, Fundamental of Guerrilla Warfare (New York: Frederick A Praeger, 1965), pp. 23-24.
39. P.N. Gabosky, "The Urban context of Political Terrorism" in Michael Stohl, *The Politics of Terrorism* (New York: Marcel.Dekker Inc., 1979) p.53.
40. Julien Paget, *Counter-Insurgency Campaign* (London : Faber and Faber, 1967), p.22.
41. Brian Cozier, *The Rebels*, op.cit., p. 15.
42. Oley Zinan, "Terrorism and Violence in the light of a Theory of Discontent and Frustration" in Brian Crozier, *The Rebels*, op.cit., p.240.
43. Hadley Centril, *The Politics of Despair* (New York: The Basic Books Inc., 1958), p.239.
44. Ted Robert Gurr, *Why Men Rebel* (New Jersey: Princeton University Press, 1970), p.24.
45. Ibid., p.24.
46. Richard H. Shultz, "The Low Intensity Conflict Environment of the 1990's", *Annals of American Association of Political Science*, 517 (September, 1991), p.125.
47. Ibid., p.108.
48. Willy Brandt, *North-South Dialogue* (London: Pan Book Ltd., 1980), p.13.
49. Paul Wilkinsom, *Political Terrorism*, op.cit., p.80.
50. Richard Clutterback, *Living with Terrorism* (New York: Arlingdon House Publishers, 1975), p.42.
51. Jenney Teichman, "How to define Terrorism", op.cit., p.510.
52. Y. Dror, *Crazy States* (New York: Millwood, 1980), p.34. Also see, John F. Murphy, *State Supported International Terrorism* (Bouldon:

Westview Press, 1989); Ved Marwah, "Role of Terrorism in Foreign-Policy", *Times of India* (New Delhi), 23 July 1992.

53. Martha Crenshaw Hutchinson "Transactional Terrorism and WorldPolitics", *Jerusalem Journal of International Relations*, Vol.1, No.2, (Winter 1975), p. 110.

54. Robert O. Keohance and Joseph S. Nye, *Transnational Relations and World Politics* (Massachusetts: Harward University Press, 1973), p.XII.

55. Edward Mickolus, "Transnational Terrorism" in Michael Stohl, *Politicsol Terrorism*, op.cit., pp.147-90.

56. David S. Carlton and Carlo Shaerif, *International Terrorism and World Security*, op.cit., p.38.

57. Andrew Smith, *Against Every Human Law: Terrorist Threat to Diplomacy* (Sydney: Australian National University, 1988), p.31.

58. David S. Carlton, *International Terrorism and World Security*, op.cit., p.40.

59. *India Today*, (New Delhi), 30 April 1989, p.29.

60. Ajsir Karim, Maj Gen (retd.), *Counter-Terrorism* (New Delhi: Lancer Publications, 1991).

Chapter 3

Terrorism and Foreign Policy

In spite of the fact that nation-states denounce the use of terrorism as an instrument of foreign policy, its application in international relations is quite obvious. Various tactics of terrorism like conspiracy, sabotage, hostage-taking, kidnapping, hijacking, logistic and financial support have been used by sovereign states to achieve their foreign policy objectives. In other words, nations are hypocritical when it comes to terrorism; they cover up their own involvement but accuse others. For instance, the U.S. labeled Libya, Syria, Iran, Lebanon, Cuba, Afghanistan and others as states sponsoring international terrorism. It is true that these countries have sponsored terrorism far and wide to achieve their respective foreign policy goals. On the other hand, U.S. foreign policy analysts purposely ignore Pakistan's active involvement in sponsoring terrorism in India because it suits their foreign policy objectives in this region at this point in time. When the situation in further deteriorated, and directly affected U.S. interests e.g. bombing of the U.S. embassy in Kenya, (1998) then U.S. policy makers realized the Pak-Afghan Mujahideen agenda of terrorism. Still the U.S. does not have any immediate plan to label Pakistan a terrorist state. The prejudice of U.S. foreign policy makers is well manifested in branding Libya, Syria, Iran and Afghanistan as terrorist states while remaining tight lipped on Pakistan. A country that does not toe the American line and challenges its authority is likely to be black listed as an evildoer. Nevertheless, if the same evildoer serves U.S. interests (such as Pakistan's overnight marriage to the U.S. after the September 11, 2001, events,) they are left free. The same is applicable to Libya and all the nations branded as terrorist by the U.S. These nations have been officially receiving arms and defense equipments from Russia, France and other technologically advanced countries rather than from the U.S. which was the main cause of American anguish.

It is relevant to mention here that Americans themselves sold Qaddafi, often at tremendous profit, the tools of terror and subversion. They lobbied in their own capital for remission of the embargoes that the Ford and the Carter administrations had imposed on U.S. military-related exports to Libya. These actions helped spread the myth that the U.S. government; long after anti-Qaddafi plots, remained more or less an acknowledged ally and good friend of the Libyan Colonel.[1] The real confrontation between the U.S. and Libya started with the treaty between Libya and France in 1976 for the sale of mirage fighter planes. This incident annoyed the U.S. to a great extent, which ultimately proved to be a turning point in U.S.-Libya relations.[2] Simultaneously application of terror tactics by Qaddafi's mercenary forces in Egypt and Chad, and active support to Palestinian militants further aggravated the situation. The relations between the two were eventually completely shattered. Besides, President Reagan had a personal fixation against Qaddafi's aggressive attitude. A bomb explosion at La Belle Disco in West Berlin, where U.S. service personnel were frequent visitors, precipitated Reagan's wrath on Libya though the investigations of the European police suspected Syria' s involvement in this incident. But the Reagan administration put the blame on Qaddafi and subsequently attacked Libya on April 15, 1986.[3] This action by the U.S. could be well described by some as an act of terrorism.

Thus, this section of the book analyses the problems of international conflict and the application of terrorism to achieve foreign policy objectives. It examines different forms of terrorism employed by nation-states in different situations.

ANALYSIS OF TERRORISM IN FOREIGN POLICY

The hypothesis that terrorism has emerged as an instrument of foreign policy needs to be examined in a proper perspective i.e. to analyze the status quo of terrorism within the broader frame of foreign policy. It is important to highlight the circumstances and compulsions of a nation that lead towards the use of terrorism to achieve its foreign policy goals. This could be analyzed by a review of different situations in foreign policy making of a nation. These situations can be classified into three categories. These are as follows:

(a) With friendly nations
(b) With belligerent nations, and
(c) With nations friendly in form and hostile in character.

Under the first category, i.e. foreign policy with friendly nations, the normal course of diplomacy is applicable, whereas in the second category, i.e. relations with belligerent nations, war or open confrontation is the determining factor. Under this situation, foreign policy objectives are realized through declared war.

However, since the world is passing through an era of political transition, nation-states find it difficult to opt for overt confrontation (with the exception of the U.S.). After the disintegration of the Soviet Union, the U.S. government is using declared war as an instrument to achieve foreign policy goals, and in doing so, it manipulates provisions of the UN to sanction its interests, e.g. the 1991 Gulf War against Iraq for the liberation of Kuwait. But the bombing of Sudan and Afghanistan by the Clinton administration in retaliation to the bombings of the U.S. Embassies in Kenya and Tanzania had no sanction as such. These actions defied international law even if they had moral sanction. Except for the U.S., normally nation-states don't use war as an instrument in the contemporary international scenario. An overt confrontation would have a far-reaching impact on long-term foreign policy options. The U.S. being the single dominant power can use war as an instrument, but other developing and developed nations cannot exercise this option. Thus, when a government has to deal with hostile countries, it has to explore a third option. Under this situation, i.e. when nations are neither friendly, nor belligerent, but have been nurturing grievances, a government can adopt terrorism as an instrument to achieve foreign policy objectives. In other words, states unable or unwilling to wage war with their adversary fight in peacetime through tactics of terrorism.[4] This situation has emerged as an important phenomenon in world politics when relations between sovereign states are more bellicose than peaceful.[5]

METHODS OF ITS APPLICATION
The forms and methods of terrorism as employed in foreign policy instruments vary from nation to nation. Broadly speaking there are

three types of Modus Operandi through which states apply terrorism to achieve foreign policy objectives,

(a) Covert Application
(b) Overt Application, and
(c) Counter Application.

It is necessary to note that the present study accepts all the three as acts of terrorism and as such, there should not be any ambiguity as to which state could be branded as terrorist. The modes of operation are based on the convenience of the nations. There are different ways employed by different nations according to their situation. The nature and purpose remain the same, be it a non-sponsored mercenary group or a government sponsored counter terrorism force.

Covert Application
Covert application is the first stage of the use of terrorism in foreign policy. It is the most important form of state-sponsored terrorism. As mentioned earlier, any act of terrorism by states defy the Geneva Convention on diplomatic relations among nations. All the signatories of the UN Charter are officially and morally bound to respect the UN Charter that clearly prescribes that nations follow a policy of non-interference and maintain territorial integrity of one another. Obviously, the member nations need to self-restrain and should not intervene in the affairs of one another. Practically, however, the situation doesn't remain so. Nations get involved in multiple bilateral and multilateral problems that affect foreign policy and intervene in the affairs of one another, specifically in relation with neighboring and hostile countries. Since they cannot afford to interfere overtly they do it covertly. For instance, Pakistan's training of Kashmiri militants and Afghan Mujahiddeens and sending them into Indian territories violates international law. The covert operation, however, continues unabetted.

A sovereign state normally does not defy set international norms abruptly as it might have adverse impact on its foreign policy. Covert operations are practiced by nation-states because they work both ways. By employing covert warfare a nation escapes criticism from the international community but simultaneously carries out acts of terrorism to achieve its goal. The global and regional powers of the world conduct covert operations and sponsor terrorism to promote their interests because these are less costly, less risky[6] than direct conflict; and are deniable too. The developing countries also use these tactics. They too have scores to settle with neighboring countries. Thus, gradually the entire international political system is affected by covert application of terrorism. This aspect will be analyzed in detail in the later part of the study discussing the role of intelligence agencies.

Overt Application

Unlike covert application, overt use of terrorism is not common in international relations. This form of terrorism is not as effective as covert operation. Overt application is bound to be condemned by nation-states and the accused country might have to bear the brunt of economic sanctions and diplomatic isolation, which is a difficult proposition in an era of global inter-dependence. But since the devices and tactics of terrorism are easily accessible to nation-states they get inclined to employ overt terrorism in their relations with unfriendly nations. The case of Libyan adventure during the 1980s is the best example of this situation. After having captured political power from King Idris in 1969, Qaddafi aspired to challenge the superpower dominance in the world through his personal military valor and stockpile of arms and ammunition (which quite tactfully he managed to horde from the U.S., France and the Soviet Union). With the help of CIA agents he established a network of subversive groups. [7] In his visionary approach to identify the Palestinian problem with the Arab's in general, (and also because of too much American interference in Middle-East politics), he terrorized the international community to such an extent that his name became synonymous with terrorism during the 1980s. The shootout from the Libyan embassy in London, killing one British police constable and the subsequent claim of immunity under the Vienna Convention on Diplomatic Relations[8] is an obvious example of overt use of terrorism.

Overt application of terrorism is adopted only when covert use fails to achieve foreign policy objectives. Generally, it is used by an aggressive state. In other words, a nation that has already decided to confront a belligerent state employs the overt form of terrorism to settle disputes. Overt use of terrorism is the first phase towards an open war. A nation opts for declared war only when all the means including overt use of terrorism fail to achieve its foreign policy goals. For example, the Clinton administration did attempt to covertly eliminate Osama Bin Laden and his compatriots, who were protected by the Taliban in Afganistan, but failed due to lack of intelligence on the ground in Afghanistan. Thus after the World Trade Center and the Pentagon attacks, the U.S. did not hesitate to declare war on Afghanistan to achieve its goal in fighting terrorism.

This form of terrorism, however, is not popular among nations. There are two major problems in its application. First, it violates international law, thus subjecting the nation to harsh measures like economic sanctions and diplomatic boycott. Second, it is an expensive affair. Very few countries can afford expenses for overt application of terrorism, as it demands preparation for war, which only rich and advanced nations can indulge in. Thus this method is not in vogue. Nations being signatories of the UN Charter that regulates code of conduct don't go that far. Only a powerful and wealthy government can adopt such an approach towards problems in international relations, but notably there are very few countries governed by dictators in the 21st-century world. Hence, overt application of terrorism is not in common practice, as it might boomerang causing immense harm to foreign policy goals rather than achieving them. The case of Col. Qaddafi's adventure could be taken as illustration of the same situation.

Counter Application

The saying, "one knell drives the other" has inspired many countries to adopt counter-terrorism policy to combat the growing menace of violence and terrorism in international politics. But these nations have overlooked another proverb, i.e. "hatred begets hatred"; which is one of the important aspects in dealing with terrorism as roots of terrorism lie more in the psychology and economic conditions than the logistic, and infrastructure they receive from across the borders. As a matter of fact, terrorism is a problem of conflict in human relationships, and a solution to such problems needs more strategic human thinking than mere use of force and violence. The best way to fight terrorism is to prevent it from happening, i.e. to eliminate the causes.

However, since nation-states are not able to eliminate causes rooted in the social and economic conditions of individuals and their society, the only policy option available to government is counter-terrorism. Social and economic problems are too deep to be rooted out quickly. It needs feasible long-term plans that could work along with a counter-terrorism policy for a lasting solution to the problems of terrorism. Apparently, countries affected by international terrorism are confronted with a complex situation. It is because of these circumstances that a nation has to adopt a policy to control terrorism. In the name of socio-economic deprivation, or some interpretation of a religion. A government cannot allow a group of people to indulge in indiscriminate killing and destruction of public properties. Thus, in the given situation, the most viable policy option is that of counter-terrorism.

The origin of counter-terrorism tactics by states could be traced back to the colonial era. During the early 19th century counter terrorism was employed by governments to suppress liberation movements. But their repression remained confined to frontiers of the colonial regime. As a tool of foreign policy, counter-terrorism rose to prominence with the rise of Communism in Southeast Asia and also because of the Palestine-Israel crisis in the Middle East during the late 20th century. In a pursuit to establish Communist hegemony, states employed counter-terror tactics to influence foreign policy of Southeast and Far East Asian countries. Vietnam and Kampuchea could be taken as good examples where government used terrorism to maintain the Communist dominance. The counter measures adopted by them had good results and gradually several non-communist states too employed counter-terrorism as a policy to combat terrorism.

Among the non-communist states, Israel and the U.S. are best known for application of counter terrorism. In so far as Israel is concerned, its actions against Palestine are well known. It uses all forms of terrorism—covert, overt and counter—against Palestinians to avenge Israeli deaths in their war of attrition. The April 1973 raid by Mivath Elohim (God's Wrath), an Israeli terror squad which killed three Palestinian guerrilla leaders in Beirut and used assassination squads to hunt and kill Palestinians is an instance of counter terrorism.[9] In 2001 there were many reports of Israeli forces striking Palestinian interests.

The U.S. strategy on counter-terrorism, though based on the same tough line approach,[10] is different from Israel. The U.S. government adopted systematic use of counter-terrorism to achieve foreign policy objectives. These measures include policy of firmness towards terrorism, exerting pressure on the states supporting terrorism and actions to deter, apprehend, and to punish terrorists.[11] One example of successful implementation of counter-terror tactics by a government is the U.S. bombing of Qaddafi's residence in 1986 in which the latter lost his adopted daughter. Though the U.S. action violated the UN charter, the former did achieve one of its foreign policy objectives i.e. to silence Qaddafi. After the bombing Qaddafi lost interest in active international politics. Maintaining the same policy, the U.S. government, in retaliation to the bombing of the U.S. embassy in Kenya launched air attacks on the bases of Osama Bin Laden's training camps in Afghanistan and Sudan in August 1998. The bombing would definitely affect future plans of the Mujahiddeen led by Bin Laden. As this study was going to press, the U.S. was again engaged in a full scale war against Afghanistan which the U.S. accuses of hosting and supporting Al-Qa'eda, the terrorist group that allegedly carried out the attacks on the WTC and the Pentagon.

This trend in international relations has encouraged several victim nations, to consider immediate response to threats posed by terrorism than to develop plans for the future.[12] However, the response option cannot work for every nation. For instance, it would be difficult for the government of India to adopt a policy of counter-terrorism in the same way that the U.S. adopted to counter attacks sponsored by Qaddafi and Al-Qa'eda. A developing country with a poor economy cannot venture into direct action as it is bound to boomerang. India, or for that matter most developing countries, can only use counter-terrorism within their national boundary to counter terrorism. Economic and political conditions of developing countries are not favorable to sustain economic sanctions and diplomatic isolation for a long period that could result from such activities.

Hence, counter-terrorism to achieve foreign policy goals is not a viable instrument in so far as India and other developing countries are concerned. Though the U.S. government is keen to tie up India in its counter-terrorism foreign policy agenda for South Asia, India needs to deal cautiously with the U.S. in matters of regional conflict in the Indian sub-continent. Osama Bin Laden's forces could be eliminated by Indian police and defense forces. India does not require U.S. assistance to do this job. However, it would not be in India's best interests to go and fight in Afghanistan. Let the U.S. deal with Osama Bin Laden and the Taliban with Pakistan. India should approve of any counter terrorism action program by the U.S. in Afghanistan, but should not participate unless it includes action in Pakistan as well. In the current situation, Afghanistan is just a pawn in the hands of Pakistani politicians and generals. India's threat emanates directly from Pakistan and not Afghanistan. India's participation in any U.S. venture exclusively against Afghanistan would damage India's long-term interests in this region.

It is obvious that terrorism is practiced by nation-states in different forms at different phases in their foreign policy. Depending on circumstances nations employ covert, overt and counter-terrorism as per their convenience and interests in international politics.

GENESIS OF STATE-SPONSORED TERRORISM

Conscious use of terror tactics in international relations is called state-sponsored terrorism, which includes both state sponsorship and direct involvement. These are not different forms of state terrorism, but two sides of the same phenomenon through which a nation-state realizes its foreign policy goal against a supposedly hostile government.

State-sponsored terrorism is defined as use of terror tactics by a nation-state to achieve certain political objectives. In the present study, all three forms—covert, overt and counter-terrorism—are clubbed together. If a state employs any of the three, it should be recognized as a terrorist state and their acts of violence as state-sponsored terrorism. In order to have proper perspective on state-sponsored terrorism, a brief historical review is necessary. Thus, study of this phenomenon could be broadly divided into two categories: (a) Historical Review and (b) Cause Factor Analysis.

Historical Review

Genesis of state terrorism could be traced back to the Reign of Terror in France during the short-lived government of Robespiere.[13] For the first time the word "terror" was used to describe the tyranny of Robespiere. It notably disappeared soon from French politics, but left imprints on political ideology of succeeding generations and foreign policy decision making of nation-states. Its importance, however, was realized during the early 20th century when configuration of major power took place during World War I in 1914 and World War II in 1939. Prior to this, terrorism and Low Intensity Conflicts (LIC) didn't exist in the same form as it exists today.

Prior to the 20th century, acts of violence and terrorism by states were in the form of repression within national boundary or had manifestation in an open war. LIC and violence were not in use during those days. It was only after the end of the two world wars that the idea of surrogate warfare[14] became an important instrument to achieve foreign policy goals of nation-states.

The government of the National Socialist or Nazis in Germany provides a classic example of this phenomenon. The Nazis could not forget the humiliating defeat in World War I. Their ego of racial supremacy was totally shattered, and they were determined to restore it. Thus, one of the most important objectives of the Nazi government in Germany was to take revenge. Hitler was convinced that the Germans were pure Aryans and deserved to rule over the world. Under this conviction, foreign policy decisions were made to prove German supremacy. In order to do so Hitler decided to eliminate all those opposed to the Nazi Government, i.e. the Jews. He used all possible means to eliminate the Jewish community. Humiliation of defeat in World War I and a superiority complex of being a community of high race destined to rule over inferiors like Jews (as Nazis considered them) inspired Hitler to use force and violence against the Jews and all anti-Nazi forces, not only within the country but all over Eastern Europe. Concentration Camps were set up throughout the region and thousands of Jews were massacred by the Nazi Government.[15] This horrifying phenomenon continued until the death of Hitler and the end of World War II in 1945.

Though the war came to an end, heinous crimes committed by the Nazis against Jews had far reaching impact on international politics during the post-war era. With the defeat of the axis power and later developments, the world politics ushered into a new phase. While on one hand, the allied powers proved their military strength and superiority over the axis power (Germany, Japan and Italy), the rise of Communism in China and in the Eastern European countries under the influence of Soviet leadership divided the world into two ideological blocks, the West and the East. In spite of the fact that the Soviet Union was with Allied powers during World War II, the post-war political developments witnessed ideological differences between the West and the Eastern European countries. In the gradual course of time, this situation led to the downfall of European colonial empires in the Afro-Asian countries and emergence of the U.S. and the Soviet Union as the superpowers, representing two ideologies, free democracy and totalitarian communism respectively.

Meanwhile, the 1948 Communist revolution in China and division of Korea on ideological lines gave impetus to growing strength of Communist governments. Emergence of Communist forces, at this stage, was well recognized. Race for armament increased and the U.S. and the Soviet Union were all set to defend their ideologies and spheres of influence. The confrontation between the two superpowers, thus, became inevitable. However, the option for an open war against the Soviet Union or the U.S. on the ground of ideological divide was against the UN Charter. Obviously, they had no alternative but to restrain their activities within the prescribed international norms. It was at this stage that they indulged in LIC and covert actions. It is important to mention that in their pursuit to achieve foreign policy goals, the superpowers did not opt direct interference but used a third nation to sponsor terrorism and hired terrorist groups, as this strategy protected them against allegation from international organizations.

Systematic use of terrorism as an instrument of foreign policy, for the first time was employed by the Communist states. The philosophy of violence is deeply rooted in Communism. It was not just the Soviet Union and China but even less powerful Communist countries used terrorism to achieve their foreign policy goals. However, the former Soviet Union, being the leader of Communist expansionism, had much more to contribute to state-sponsored terrorism than China or other Communist countries. During the 1960s and 1970s, the Soviet government used developing countries that had inclinations towards communist ideology. The entire Eastern European countries came under the Soviet influence. These counties were used as pawns to achieve Soviet foreign policy goals, e.g. expansion of the Communist empire and to increase areas of influence. China and Cuba also used terrorism as an instrument to achieve their foreign policy goals in South Asia and Latin America respectively. Mass political violence and unrest in Kampuchea and Vietnam during the 1960s and 1970s was the consequence of Chinese assistance to insurgents in this region. Similarly, Cuba also played an active role in abetting terrorism for the cause of Soviet Communism.

With the rise and success of Communism, democratic countries also adopted terrorism to accomplish their goals in international politics. Having experienced the success of Communist powers, they too realized the relevance of terrorism in international politics. In the name of counter-measures, the U.S. and several other democratic nations employed terror tactics as bargaining power to settle long-standing disputes. The U.S. interference in the political affairs of the Latin American countries could be defined as conscious use of terror tactics to destabilize Communist countries in this region. During the post-World War II era, the U.S. and other democratic countries seriously felt the need to combat expansion of Communism. When the economic compulsions of the third world democratic countries did not let them adopt an aggressive policy, the U.S. and other developed nations did use terrorism as an instrument.

One of the important factors behind the use of terrorism by democratic governments is its liberal character. A liberal society is a warehouse of freedom. People enjoy so much freedom that at times it is misused. They tend to use violence and terror tactics to get their demands fulfilled. Agitation and mass movement are essential tools for the success of a democratic society. People take advantage of this situation. In order to achieve their political objective, a few groups adopt violence and terror and when they fail to gain a sufficient support system from within the country, they establish contact across the border. A democratic government finds it difficult to deal with such groups, and therefore, is compelled to use counter-terrorism. At times, they contact foreign agencies for assistance that further complicates the situation for the government. Under such circumstances, the victim nation is compelled to adopt counter-terrorism.

Furthermore, terrorism affects both the domestic and the foreign policy of nations-states. While special legislations are formulated and implemented to cope with the crisis within the domestic frontiers, the foreign policy is influenced because of international connection of militant groups. Thus, the use of terrorism that started with the ideological conflict between the superpowers during the Cold War era, has now become a subject of common concern. Crossing all the ideological lines, terrorism has emerged as a viable alternative to war towards the realization of foreign policy goals of nation-states. The case of Pak-sponsored terrorism in India could be taken as an example. As a matter of fact, with the break up of the Soviet Union and its Eastern European Communist empire, ideology, i.e. communism, has lost its importance. Had it (ideology) been the only reason for the use of terrorism, it would have ceased to exist after the disintegration of the former Soviet Union. However, the situation did not change. Obviously ideological divide was just one of the factors for the use of terrorism during the Cold War era. As a matter of fact, terrorism is a viable instrument that could be used for any purpose, viz. ideology, security, or politico-economic supremacy. There are serious compelling issues that inspire nation-states to use terrorism. The following section highlights these factors in pursuit to realization of foreign policy objectives.

Cause-Factor Analysis
There are various causes for the use of terrorism by nation-states. These causes are described here as (1) political factors and (2) economic factors.

Political Factor
The political factor could be analyzed in the light of post-World War II international relations. During the post-World War II period, global politics was divided into three blocks; (1) The U.S.-led democratic world, (2) Soviet led Communist powers, and (3) the Nonaligned group. The causes for this configuration of forces were: war ravaged economy, ideological divide, military strength, and nuclear technology. Of all these, ideological divide, military strength and nuclear capability were the dominant factors in the post-war political situation.

The ideological divide between the superpowers was complete. Both the U.S. and Soviets were all set to increase their area of influence. The global polity, thus, was mainly divided into two blocks, viz. the U.S.-led democratic world and the Soviet-led Communist power. Both of them influenced developing countries in pursuance to realization of their goals. They employed all accessible means, including violence and subversion to achieve their objectives.

It is relevant to note that normally foreign policy goals are determined on the strength of nation's armed forces and defense technology. These two factors are important in decision-making. A strong army is a potential threat to weaker armed forces, specifically, but not necessarily, of a neighboring country. Strength of armed forces generate fear psychosis among weaker nations, as they have neither strong armies nor advanced defense technology. In such situations, if a strong nation wages war, the weaker nation has no choice but to use proxy war as it can't compete with a stronger army. Since no nation can surrender simply because it lacks strength to fight, terrorism comes as an alternative to cope with such conditions.

Similarly, nuclear capability is also an important factor in the decision making of foreign policy. It has indirect repercussions on the growth of terrorism in international relations. This aspect could be analyzed in the light of the fact that if defense forces of a nation are weak but it has nuclear technology, it dominates regional politics.[16] A weak nation is likely to compromise with powerful nations. However, under no circumstances, would a nation compromise with its national interests. If it does not have the strength to fight a war, it adopts terrorism to achieve its objectives.

The nuclear factor in decision making of foreign policy could be analyzed in the light of situations wherein a nation acquires superiority over others. A non-nuclear belligerent nation avoids overt confrontation against a nuclear power. For instance, ever since India successfully tested the nuclear bomb in 1974, Pakistan switched over from direct confrontation to application of terrorism in a well-planned manner. Even after having acquired the nuclear bomb in 1998, nuclear weaponry is still a deadly and counter productive option. As a result both India and Pakistan would avoid its application. This again provides scope for Pakistan to use terrorism for settlement of disputes between the two.

At the global level, the policy of nuclear deterrence amongst the U.S., Russia, Great Britain, Germany and France, to a great extent has helped to avoid a nuclear war. But this restrain promoted international terrorism. The issues, which were earlier decided by declared war, are now being achieved through surrogate warfare and terrorism. Both the communist and the democratic countries employed terror tactics to achieve their foreign policy goals, be it related to territorial disputes in regional politics, to increase area of influence or to control oil (life line of modern civilization) at the global level. Terrorism is employed by nation-states for different purposes. The economy is one of the important aspects that dominate policy-making.

Economic Factor

To a great extent, economic interests of nation-states determine foreign policy decisions. The U.S. support of Saudi Arabia and other monarchies in the Middle East is directly connected to securing oil resources. The Russian support of Syria during the Cold War era was also aimed to achieve the same. In order to safeguard economic interests, at times nation-states, especially major powers, use terror tactics.

The economic factor in the growth of terrorism, however, could be mainly seen in foreign policy making of narcotic drug producing countries in Central America, South and Southeast Asia. Terrorist groups are a potential market for drugs produced in Columbia, Bolivia, Peru, Nicaragua, Pakistan, Afghanistan and Myanmar. Nexus between the terrorist groups and the narcotic drug producing countries is an important factor for the rise of terrorism in international politics. These countries use terrorist groups as safe channels to market their produce. Terrorists are mobile and have contacts all over the world. They carry drugs along with weapons and deliver them to prospective buyers. The terrorist groups and the government agencies sponsoring terrorism then share the proceeds of the drug sales. Latin American countries are well known for such transactions. The role of the ISI in Kashmir is also a case of the same situation. Pakistani drug syndicates fund the ISI-sponsored terrorist activities in India. The Pakistan government cannot intervene in the tribal areas of NWFP, where the local administration of the Pathan tribe protects growth of poppy cultivation, because their economy is dependent on drugs. So deep rooted is the nexus between narcotics and international terrorism that in Latin America LIC is defined as narco-terrorism and the U.S. government had to pass an act to deal with it. The same situation prevails in India. Air Commodore Jasjit Singh, defense analyst and director of IDSA, strongly holds that unless governments break the nexus of narcotic drug trafficking and terrorism, the latter cannot be curbed. He believes that proceeds from drugs are the main source of funds for terrorist activities and unless the financial source is cut, terrorism cannot be curbed.[17] The government of India realized the inherent threat and passed the

Narcotic Drug and Psychotropic Substance Act, 1985 (NDPS) to deal with the situation.

In brief, competition to control oil reserves and the business of narcotic drugs are two major economic issues that promoted terrorism in international relations. Beside these two, there are other economic factors that are already discussed earlier in the second chapter and hence need not be reiterated.

ROLE OF INTELLIGENCE AGENCIES

Relations among nations are often full of bitterness. The games nations play with one another are not chaste and naive but full of deception and treachery.

Since nation-states are restricted to a common bond of humanity and harmony, deception and espionage activities are kept secret and no government confirms that it employs these instruments in policy implementation.[18] But, there is ample evidence to confirm that nations do indulge in covert operations. In some 200 revolutions that took place during the early phase of this century, foreign intervention and under cover operation was reported in approximately 50 of these revolutions, and more than one foreign power intervened.[19] Nazi subversion of Czechoslovakia during 1938-1939, Soviet military action in the entire Eastern European block during the 1960s, and the U.S. intervention in South American countries are some of important events in contemporary history of the world that reveal the application of clandestine operations. All these revolutions received political and economic assistance from foreign lands. While Russia was active in the Eastern European countries, America played an important role in Latin America.

States that have hostile relations with neighbors or elsewhere implicitly employ subversion to achieve their goals. It is a common practice in international politics to indulge in unlawful activities and deny involvement the next day. The CIA, for instance, did consider assassinating Fidel Castro and bombarded the residence of Qaddafi, though assassination is illegal as per the CIA code.[20]

It is apparent that states do get involved in covert operations and democratic nations are no exception to this rule. Whatever might be the democratic principle, i.e. of the people, by the people and for the people (Lincoln), political system is such that transparency is not possible in diplomatic relations. States irrespective of ideology, have adopted secrecy as an essential condition to deal with domestic violence and external aggression. In an era of conflict and rivalry among nation- states, there is every justification for nations to defend their covert operations if vital national interests are threatened.[21] Intelligence plays an important role at this stage of decision making.

Intelligence as Situation Analyst

The most significant role intelligence plays in abetting or curbing terrorism is that of situation analyst. It is through these agencies that a government carries its task to curb or sponsor terrorism. These agencies are entrusted with the responsibility of making thorough analysis of law and order situation. On the basis of the feedback from intelligence agencies governments make crucial decisions to combat international terrorism. Issues such as whether the use of counter violence is justified, will it be effective or what should be the intensity of violence if employed, are of serious concern. All such issues are decided by the government at high levels, but the decision depends on competent analysis of intelligence departments. It is through these agencies that a government receives detailed information about psychological environments, changing political ideology, objectives, chances of success and overall implications of counter-terrorism operations.

Thorough research and analysis is done by intelligence agencies. During the post-World War II period, growth of intelligence agencies has increased substantially. So much that one can see two governments running parallel—visible and invisible. The invisible government gathers intelligence, conducts espionage, and executes secret operations all over the world.[22] The U.S. National Security Act of 1947 highly recommended the role of intelligence in functioning of government agencies. This act made the CIA, at that point in time, more powerful compared to any other intelligence agencies in the world.[23] The need for intelligence has grown so much that the CIA, which used to be number one, has become less effective compared to Israel's MOSSAD. The CIA and the KGB were popular during the post-World War II period. But British M15 and M16, French services of External Documentation and Counter Espionage (SDECE) and Israel's MOSSAD are no less than these two. Since conflict is a regular phenomenon in international politics, developing countries also use their intelligence agencies to achieve foreign policy goals. RAW in India, SAVAK in Iran and ISI (Inter-Service Intelligence) in Pakistan are among the active intelligence agencies in the world. But the CIA (the KGB is defunct after the disintegration of the former Soviet Union)[24] and MOSSAD have no parallel because these two are well equipped with sophisticated communication systems and members are trained according to the changing situations. Besides, the CIA and MOSSAD have no dearth of funds, whereas intelligence agencies in developing countries have to operate under financial constraints. The need for secret information became so imminent that one of the British Intelligence officers associated with M15 said that the Cold War will be fought with spies, not soldiers.[25] A thorough analysis of circumstances leading towards the disintegration of the Soviet Communist empire and the end of the Cold War supports this hypothesis. The Reagan administration used intelligence agencies to extensively monitor political developments in the former Soviet Union. The mess created by the socialist economy was exposed by the CIA to gain political mileage, which gradually caused disintegration of the USSR and the end of the Cold War between the superpowers. Similarly, intelligence has a bigger role to play in state-sponsored terrorism or use of violence by states during conflict than during peacetime. This aspect is significant because terrorism by an individual or a group does not raise as many brows across the border as state-sponsored terrorism does. Use of terrorism by a state in a systematic manner has direct implications on foreign policy making of others. Thus utmost precision is needed while making such crucial decisions. In order to avoid adverse implications that might arise if counter-terrorism is adopted, the government takes intelligence agencies into confidence. And as such, intelligence plays an important role in the decision-making process. For instance, it is now public knowledge that one reason the Clinton administration could not get Osama Bin Laden was the lack of intelligence information from the ground in Afghanistan. The Bush administration's pursuit of terrorists in Afghanistan is more successful, in part, because of intelligence information from the Northern Alliance fighting to topple the Taliban and, obviously, also from Pakistan's ISI.

Intelligence in Decision Making

Since intelligence agencies are well informed and equipped with the latest communication technology, they are well positioned to disseminate information and keep governments abreast of the situation. Intelligence agencies have direct access to people and their environment. Some information is vital to the nation. Lack of accuracy could be detrimental, more so in use of terrorism. Intelligence agencies get directly involved in the affairs of terrorism, be it for sponsoring or countering. They are always there in field operations and are the main source of information to the government. Another advantage of intelligence agency is its official interactions with the global network of intelligence.[26] Because of official contacts with other intelligence agencies, specially those equipped with more sophisticated skills in espionage, their analysis is more accurate compared to other sources of information. Vital decisions of government are normally made on the basis of intelligence report specifically those concerning national security.

In consultation with defense forces, intelligence agencies recommend strategic locations to check infiltration of terrorists crossing borders. It also participates in planning counter-terrorism. Apathy to intelligence reports might prove costly for a government. Operation Blue Star (1984) in Punjab is an example of government apathy towards intelligence. The intelligence department of the government of India repeatedly reported that the terrorists are hiding and hoarding arms and ammunition within the premises of the Golden Temple in Amritsar. But the government showed apathy to the reports. The matter that could have been resolved by police action had to be dealt with militarily in the Golden Temple causing anguish, pain and psychological alienation of the Sikh community during the 1980s. This could have been averted had the Congress government taken intelligence reports seriously and adopted counter-terrorism in advance. Similarly, Pakistan's venture at Kargil and Drass sectors in Kashmir in June 1999 could have been averted if the government had taken intelligence agencies' reports seriously.

It is relevant to note here that if intelligence agencies function under political influence, as it happens and has happened in many countries especially under totalitarian and communist regimes, there is the risk that the information provided might be concocted in favor of the ruling government. A classis example of this phenomenon is the erstwhile Soviet Union. The USSR intelligence agency was headed by one of the premiers. Before becoming President, Yuri Andropov was the Chairman of the KGB. Similarly, the CIA, MOSSAD, ISI and many others have political affiliation. It is relevant to note that political influence on intelligence agencies is not a positive trend, it might have adverse impact on national interests of the country. It sets a dangerous trend and can jeopardize security of the nation concerned. Under such circumstances, decisions by the government can boomerang specifically in the case of dealing with international terrorism. The fact, however, remains that whether concocted in favor of the ruling party or otherwise intelligence plays an important role in state-sponsored terrorism. The effective role of Pakistan's intelligence agencies in sponsoring terrorism in India is analyzed at length in the next chapter.

TYPES OF STATES USING TERRORISM

States use terror tactics to achieve foreign policy goals with the help of intelligence agencies. In the beginning there were few to acknowledge this new trend in international relations. Policy makers considered it as propaganda by terrorist groups to create public opinion in their favor and an obscure idea in the realm of international polity. But with the passage of time, sponsoring as well as direct involvement of states in abetting terrorism has become a matter of serious concern. The changing scenario during the post-World War II period confirms that patronage and support of terrorism would be a minor annoyance rather than a global problem of expanding dimensions.[27] Terror tactics as used by patrons were considered useful to many nations during the 1970s.[28] A number of governments provided terrorists safe haven, travel documents, arms training, and technical expertise. In addition, some governments became directly engaged in terrorism as a tool to implement their foreign policies.[29]

There has been too much hue and cry about types of states employing violence and terrorism. While western democratic nations accuse communist or totalitarian states as the culprits; the latter accuse the former of the same. But the fact remains that both have employed terrorism to achieve their foreign policy goals. The only difference, if there exists any, is that of time. Democratic nations began to use terrorism much later compared to the Communists; and as a corollary to this, it is important to mention that circumstances under which democratic states use terrorism vary from that of the Communists. A comparative study of both would help us understand circumstances under which totalitarian and democratic states use terrorism to achieve their foreign policy goals.

Use of Terrorism by Totalitarian States

As mentioned earlier, totalitarian states were the first to use violence and repressive measures in international politics. Beginning with the fascists in Italy, Nazis in Germany, to the Communists in Russia and China during the 20th Century, application of terrorism has been in practice. The rise of Communism, the most recent form of dictatorial government, and Marx's call for the workers of the world to unite against the capitalist forces, gave impetus to the growth of Communist forces in the world. As a result, the linkage of Communist states with revolutionary groups fighting for the cause of the working class throughout the world became well recognized. Communist regimes like Russia and China maintained considerable influence on these groups and provided moral, financial, political and logistic support to all those working for the cause of Communism. Since Communism believes in the ideology of force and violence as important means to achieve political and economic goals, Communist countries used terrorism in a systematic manner. In the beginning, violence is used to achieve political or economic gains; it continues in order to consolidate the accomplished objectives. And lastly, its application is further extended in order to intimidate potential opponents.[30]

Led by the former Soviet Union, most of the Communist states shared a common platform for expansion of Communism by terror tactics. Communist International became very active with political and economic support of powerful Communist governments like the former Soviet Union and China. Members and agents of the Communist International were sent to conspire and instigate people for revolution against the established governments.

The former Soviet government acquired immense political and economic power over Communist countries.[31] The Soviet Union signed innumerable treaties with Eastern European countries like Czechoslovakia, Romania, Hungary, Poland, Bulgaria and others to acquire official sanction over its political design. These countries were used as agents and instruments to achieve Soviet foreign policy goals in Europe. Furthermore, the government extended economic, political, military and ideological support to several revolutionary groups fighting for liberation from the British, French, Portuguese, Spanish and American domain in Asia, Africa and America during the 60s, 70s and 80s. This support was more vigorous in the countries where the chances of victory for Communist groups were fairer than the liberal or the right wing political parties. In order to achieve this objective, training camps were set up in Tashkent as part of the Third International agenda to aid and assist Afro-Asian colonies fighting against imperial rule. Lenin openly announced that the struggle against capitalism would be a global revolutionary effort. He made it explicitly clear that these efforts included military training, political agitation and propaganda techniques.[32] As part of this agenda, Soviet leader, Khrushchev gave utmost importance to revolutionary groups to achieve foreign policy goals.

The overthrow of General Batiste in Cuba by Fidel Castro in 1959 is an example of the same policy adopted by the totalitarian regime of the Soviet Union. Logistic support to Algeria, PLO, Syria, Libya and other Middle East countries was part of the same design. The Cuban foreign policy under the leadership of Castro too toed the Soviet ideological line. Not only in neighboring Latin America, but also in far flung African countries like Angola. Cuba has been exporting terror tactics in a well-planned manner to subvert any political game by the West-led capitalist powers. However, it is relevant to note that after the disintegration of Soviet Russia, the trend has changed precisely because communism is no longer considered an alternative to capitalism.

Notwithstanding the fact that nations do use means of terrorism to settle their regional disputes, specifically that of a territorial nature, it is relevant to mention that not all the totalitarian states have Communist governments. Though not under Communism, military regimes in different parts of the world like Latin America, the Middle East and Africa are equally repressive and use terror tactics to remain in power specifically in a situation when they find a democratic country interfering in their domestic affairs.

Use of Terrorism by Democratic States

It is easy to brand a totalitarian state as terrorist. But it is not just the totalitarian states that use terrorism. Whenever the need for application of terror tactics arises, nation-states employ it to achieve their foreign policy goals, be it totalitarian or democratic regimes. Use of terrorism by democratic states is more in the form of counter-terrorism. Unlike totalitarian governments that believe in inflicting violence to expand their area of influence or to protect their regimes, democratic states use violence and terror tactics to counter the same. Indiscriminate killing and repression are incompatible with the liberal values of humanity, liberty and justice,[33] the fundamental principles of democracy. Democratic states generally do not use violence unless vital issues are at stake and there is valid reason to justify use of terror in international relations.

Since democratic states are more liberal than totalitarian ones, they are the most likely targets of terrorist activities and this is why most of the democratic countries are victims of international terrorism. Uruguay is an example of the same situation.

Uruguay, once known as a model Latin American democracy had to experience constant use of violence and terrorism inflicted by the Tupamaros, the most dreaded terrorist group in Uruguay.[34] The Tupamaros completely destroyed the democratic structure of the country. The break up of the system brought military dictatorship that eliminated the Tupamaros. By digging the grave of liberal democracy in Uruguay, the Tupamaros ultimately dug their own grave.[35]

Democracy is highly prone to international terrorism and hence has to adopt certain measures to curb it; it is at this stage that a democratic nation uses counter-terrorism. It needs to be emphasized that not all terror tactics used by a democratic state are counter-terrorism. There are quite a good number of democratic nations using such instruments to settle ideological or territorial disputes, for instance, use of violence and terrorism by the democratically elected government of Israel against the PLO. Israel, however, is just one of the various examples of terrorism practiced by democratic states in international relations.

Of all the democratic countries the U.S. is the most discredited nation to have used counter-terrorism in various parts of the world through its intelligence and diplomatic missions abroad. Along with the U.S., a host of other small democratic countries also have been using various tactics and methods of international terrorism to accomplish their foreign policy goals. The U.S. being the democratic superpower and at present the single dominant power in the world uses counter-terrorism more systematically than others. Their diplomatic missions function in communion with that of the CIA and other intelligence agencies. The concern for counter-terrorism action was so serious that President Kennedy gave full power to the chiefs of diplomatic missions to use their discretionary power to protect U.S. interests. He wrote "the mission includes not only the personnel of the Department of State and Foreign Service, but also the representatives of all other agencies[36] which have program or activities ..."[37] All the censured parts of the letter, actually referred to counter-terrorism operations.[38] Maintaining the same approach, the Reagan administration issued a warning in aggressive language that the U.S. would hit back hard against terrorists and the states sponsoring terrorism. So high was Reagan's enthusiasm that during his first term of office, he spent more time on the details of covert activities than any of his predecessors.[39]

However, it was not President Reagan who was solely responsible for employing covert operations. Long before Reagan came to power, the U.S. Congress enacted a law in 1974 that was approved by the Senate. The bill, S.1721, among other aspects, also included a provision which authorizes the executive branch to conduct "special activities" if the President decides them to be necessary to support foreign policy objectives.[40] Because of volatile situations created by use of terrorism and politics of violence by the PLO and its allies during the 1970s, this legislation was enacted. Hijacking and killing had become an order of the day during this period. The U.S. and other Western protectors of Israel were the direct target of the terrorists fighting for the cause of the PLO. Because of these factors, the U.S. took to a violent course of action. And thus set the example of democratic nations' participation in counter-terrorism

Furthermore, after the disintegration of the Soviet Union, international politics have changed and the U.S. no longer uses terrorism as counter measures but goes straight to attack or declares war against any hostile nation in the name of chemical and biological weapons disarmament, terrorism and human rights. The bombing of Iraq in 1998 and Yugoslavia in 1999 are examples of the U.S. and its allies acting as global police and intimidating weaker nations to toe their line of approach to international politics. These acts could be described as overt use of terrorism.

These are obvious examples of democratic nations using terrorism to achieve their foreign policy goals. Hence it would be unfair to accuse only Communist countries for use of terrorism and acquit the democrats. The fact remains that every nation is capable of using terrorism and they use it as and when it suits their foreign policy interests.

STATE TERRORISM AND POWER RIVALRY

"Power" is the crux of this section of the study. The tactics states employ to acquire power varies from time to time and depends on the prevailing situation. This is true with every nation, big or small, democratic or communist, they all intend to capture power. The desire to capture power is the beginning of struggle for power in international relations. Rivalry for power is the most important factor of the growth of international terrorism specifically those sponsored by governments. It would be easier to understand systematic use of state-sponsored terrorism by following Model IV on "conflict in international relations."

Model IV
Conflict in International Relations

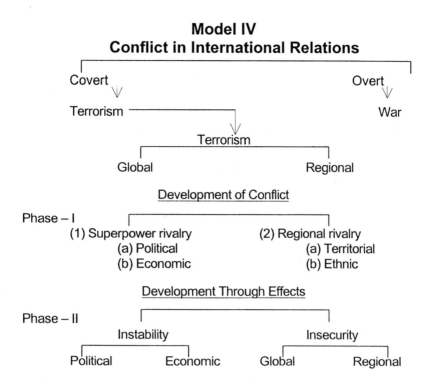

Covert		Overt
Terrorism		War

Terrorism

Global	Regional

Development of Conflict

Phase – I

(1) Superpower rivalry	(2) Regional rivalry
(a) Political	(a) Territorial
(b) Economic	(b) Ethnic

Development Through Effects

Phase – II

Instability	Insecurity

Political	Economic	Global	Regional

As per this model, confrontation in international relations could be broadly divided into two categories - covert and overt. Overt confrontation directly leads to war to which the present study is not concerned. It is relevant to mention here that confrontations overt in nature, but not declared war and the action is similar to terrorism, would be well considered as covert action, for example, armed confrontations at the international borders, i.e. deliberate infringement between armed forces of two nations or groups supported by the belligerent nation to divert attention of security guards so that terrorists can infiltrate other side of the border without much difficulty. The case of Pakistan is a good example of overt action. But it needs to be reiterated that all such acts would be analyzed along with the covert operations, which subsequently leads to terrorism.

For proper analysis of power as a factor, the study of terrorism can be divided into two broad categories, i.e. global and regional. These are the two major issues that dominate foreign policy making and influence development of conflict in international relations. Power is the center of attraction in international relations. Who and how a nation-state climbs the ladder of power determine the fate of that particular nation in global and regional politics.

Present international politics is based on inter-dependence and as such global issues have regional implications and vice-versa. International terrorism is also one of the products of conflict emanating from global and regional complexities, the thrust of which is to acquire power—political, economic or military. In the new world order, there is hardly any political issue that doesn't have global implication. For example, regional security of South Asia, nuclear testing by India, Pakistan or by China cannot be treated as regional problems. It has far reaching impact. The entire world gets concerned because national interests of many nations, particularly of the major world power, are affected. Similarly when the UN or the U.S. and its allies adopt a resolution to bomb a member nation in the pretext of saving mankind, it definitely affects the political equation of that region. For instance, the UN decision to bomb Iraq or NATO's decision to bomb Yugoslavia were events that have far reaching impact on regional politics of the Middle East and Eastern Europe respectively.

A vivid example of such complexities promoting terrorism is the U.S. decision to arm Pakistan during the 70s and 80s against the

Soviet expansion of Communism. The U.S. supplied weapons to Pakistan to check expansion of Soviet Communism, but ultimately weapons were used for terrorism in India, which resulted in overt conflict in the Indian sub-continent.

The model further highlights that development of terrorism in international relations could be divided into two categories, they are

(a)   Development of Terrorism through causes, and
(b)   Development of Terrorism through effects.

Development of Terrorism through Causes
Causes are vital for understanding terrorism, more so when it is sponsored by a state. Nations adopt terrorism as an to achieve their foreign policy goals in a situation when either its territorial integrity, security, sovereignty or ideology is threatened. Unless such issues of great national interest are included, democratic countries avoid indulging in terrorist acts. However, there are innumerable issues in international politics that affect the international community and apparently nation-states have to respond to the situation be they superpowers or regional powers. Under circumstances like this every nation tends to protect its national interest and acquires power to safeguard against future threats.

This situation creates lots of complexities in international relations as nation-states have different yardsticks to measure their national interest and ideology though they have adopted the UN Charter and agreed to all its resolutions for peaceful co-existence. As a result, there always exists the possibility of confrontation among nations, which could be of various nature and degree. In the present context, the matter of concern is confrontation that leads to state-sponsored terrorism and its causes. In other words, circumstances under which an established government uses terrorism needs to be highlighted to understand the role of terrorism in foreign policy making. Thus, the case of development of conflict that leads to terrorism could be analyzed from two perspectives, e.g. first the struggle for power at the global level among advanced nations of the world like the U.S., U.K., Germany, France, Russia, China; and second, the power rivalry at the regional level among nations to dominate regional politics in different pockets of the world.

In the first category, i.e. power rivalry among the major world powers, it is worth noting that prior to the disintegration of the USSR, the U.S. and the Communist Russia played an important role in the development of conflict in international politics that promoted growth of transnational terrorism.

Notwithstanding the fact that the USSR disintegrated and the U.S. emerged as the single dominant power in the new world order, it is relevant to mention in the present study how the two superpowers promoted terrorism in some form or the other to increase their area of influence and acquire power. The two superpowers used developing and under-developed countries to serve their foreign policy agenda and divided the world into two groups, e.g. U.S.-led democratic countries and the Soviet-led Communist states. In the process they introduced a race for armament and supplied sophisticated weapons and defense technology to their respective military bases all over the world. For instance, the U.S. used Pakistan as a base to challenge expansion of Soviet Communism. Similarly, the former Soviet Union used Syria and Lebanon in the Middle East and Cuba in the Pacific as frontline states to contain the U.S. hegemony in the post-World War II period. During the 1970s and 1980s the U.S. and the erstwhile USSR produced enormous sophisticated weapons and improved their defense technology. The stockpile of weapons was enough for a third world war. But, it worked as a deterrent and prevented the possibility of an open war between the two. Since open war was not a viable option, the U.S. and the Soviet Union used their allies in the Middle East, Southeast Asia, South Asia and Pacific countries as bases for sponsoring covert acts of terrorism.

In the same way, causes for the growth of terrorism in the regional power rivalry could be analyzed. Armed with sophisticated weapons and technology, countries used as bases during global superpower rivalry, strived to dominate over one another in regional politics. They were better equipped and had financial assistance coming from the U.S. or the USSR. This brought changes in the regional power equation and the opportunity to settle their territorial disputes. It is important to note that problems in regional politics are mainly related to territorial conflicts, though ethnic conflict also has a share in the regional power equation. But territorial conflict is a major factor in bilateral relations and regional politics.

The socio-economic conditions of developing countries are

vital determinants in regional politics. Most of these countries have similar socio-economic conditions. When a superpower supplies sophisticated weapons and provides economic assistance to one of these, the beneficiary state becomes more powerful and develops a tendency to dominate and use force to achieve its foreign policy goals in the region. In other words, they become inclined to use terrorism to settle their disputes. Syria's support of the PLO and Pakistan-sponsoring terrorism in India are examples of the same situation. While Syria received assistance from the erstwhile USSR, Pakistan received from the U.S. It is a known fact that the weapons supplied to Pakistan, Syria and others were extensively used to sponsor terrorism across the border. These are vital facts in international relations specifically in regional politics that give rise to terrorism.

Apparently, there are various issues that lead towards terrorism in international relations. Most of these originate from the continuous struggle for power at global and regional levels. All these factors, e.g. weapons, politics, economy, territorial disputes and ethnic conflict both at the global and regional level are important issues that cause transnational terrorism.

Development of Terrorism Through Effects

"Every action has its equal and opposite reaction" said Newton in the context of his scientific discovery. The same rule is applicable to international terrorism also because grievances cannot be eliminated without creating other ones.[41] This is why the cycle of violence, counter-terrorism and terrorism has come to exist as a threat to mankind. It is from this perspective that development of terrorism through effects could be analyzed.

Counter-terrorism could be described as terrorism of this kind. Counter-terrorism is a result of perpetual threat to political stability and economic security of a nation by a group of terrorists supported by neighboring or any hostile countries. Various means of terrorism like violence, arson, killing, kidnapping and hijacking are used occasionally by the hostile nation to destabilize the other. The victim nation also resorts to similar means in retaliation. This process is an example of the development of conflict through effect. This aspect of terrorism could be further divided into two categories, e.g. development of terrorism as a result of political instability, and second, as a result of global and regional insecurity

Political instability caused by state-sponsored terrorism is of two types - political and economic. When a nation passes through a phase of economic and political crisis, it directly affects its political system. Under such circumstances tremendous pressure is built on the victim nation-state both from within as well as from outside forces. Sometimes this mounting pressure results in wrong decisions by the government such as use of violence, coercion and counter-terrorism to deal with hostile forces working against the government. Such decisions might or might not serve the interest of the nation. It could prove counter-productive.

The most important aspect in development of conflict that leads to terrorism through effects is the sense of insecurity. While political and economic instability can take a nation on a violent path, a perpetual threat to the security of a nation can compel the government to use terrorism to deal with elements that cause insecurity.

The effect of insecurity leading towards terrorism too could be analyzed both from regional and global perspectives. Global insecurity is a worldwide phenomenon whereas regional insecurity is confined to the respective regions.

Global insecurity could be identified as a phenomenon that arises from non-amicable actions of major powers. The Soviet aggression of Eastern Europe during the 1960s and 1970s provides an example. These events destabilized the global political system. It brought innumerable changes in international relations. Nation-states were compelled to tie up with either of the two superpowers. Many of them took to covert operations to challenge the growing power of totalitarian states. The rivalry between the two superpowers had created a sense of global insecurity. They had economic and military superiority over developing countries. A number of these states got protection from the superpowers, and a number of them remained neutral. However, most of them had insecurity of being victims of the superpower rivalry. Some of these countries were used as bases for sponsoring covert warfare of the U.S. against the former USSR and vice verse, whereas some decided to stay neutral and defended themselves by employing covert actions against any aggression caused by superpower rivalry. In the entire process, both the superpowers and the developing countries used terrorism to defend themselves. The U.S. counter-terrorism policy to deal with the Colombian drug cartels, and Israeli and Syrian acts of terrorism in the Middle East politics could be described as growth of terrorism as consequence of superpower rivalry.

Similarly, regional powers get involved in proxy war and LIC that causes insecurity in the region. The case for use of terror tactics in this case is regional and narrow compared to the superpower rivalry. The ultimate goal, however, is the same i.e. dominance in regional politics.

During the past century we witnessed the power rivalry between communist and capitalist forces. Now that communist powers have gradually diminished, although the Chinese citadel is yet to crumble, it is likely that ultimately communism will disappear. This does not, however, indicate that international terrorism too would cease to exist.

The Cold War is over. But the end of the Cold War does not mean that the desire for power has also faded. Ideological confrontation between the U.S. and the former Soviet Union was not the only factor for the beginning of the Cold War. A candid view of the circumstances that led to the beginning of the Cold War and international terrorism do not confirm it. The superpowers had ulterior motives behind the game. The major cause for their rivalry was to establish superiority over each other especially in defense technology and economy, and thereby increasing their sphere of influence. The expansion of Soviet power over eight and one half million square mile, or on sixth of the land surface of the planet, and further expansion beyond this huge are roused serious alarm that the Soviet leaders were bent on conquering the world.[42] Events in the Balkan i.e. internationalization of Trieste and Danube, the main ports on the passage for most sea-borne imports and exports between the Balkan countries and the West, further testified that there was a tremendous sense of insecurity and suspicion.[43] These two ports locate in the Balkan region were finally freed and placed under the UN Security Council.

Furthermore, political developments in China, its emergence as a Communist power and subsequent rift in the Sino-Soviet relations on territorial and ideological issues, clearly gave signals that the Soviet Union was playing a power game to rule over the entire world. Hoffman rightly observed that "let's not talk about it as the spread of Communism, let's talk about it for what it is an attempt by the gang in the politburo to take over the world.[44]

But this phenomenon of power rivalry in international politics was not new to the former Soviet Union or the U.S. During the 20th Century it came in the guise of Communism. Prior to this we experienced the colonial power politics of Great Britain, France, Portugal, the U.S. and Japan. Expansion of the British Empire around the world is also an example of the thirst for power in the guise of trade and economic interaction.

Recent developments in the U.S. foreign policy also substantiate the argument of power as the most important factor in the growth of terrorism. While bombing of Bin Laden's base in Afghanistan could be cited as a case for overt use of counter-terrorism, i.e. terrorism through effects, bombing of Yugoslavia would be described as terrorism for a cause. In the absence of an equally strong power, the U.S. enjoys hegemony over the world. This creates an atmosphere of insecurity among nation-states. This situation too can lead towards terrorism.

Thus, it could be sufficed that power is one of the most decisive factors in international relations, which if not restricted goes to the extent of using terrorism to achieve foreign policy goals i.e to acquire political and economic power in international relations.

REFERENCES

1. John Cooley, *Libyan Sandstorm* (London: Sindgwick and Jackson, . 1983), p.83.
2. Ibid., p.160.
3. Conon Gearty, *Terror* (London: Faber & Faber, 1991), pp.83-85.
4. Kenneth E. Boulding, *Conflict and Defense* (New York: Harper and Brothers, 1962), pp. 142-4.
5. Raymond Anon, *On War* (London: Secker and Warburg, 1958), p.15.
6. Raymond Anon, *Peace and War (London:* Secker and Warburg, pp. 60-61.
7. D.M. Sehlagheck, *International Terrorism* (Massachusetts: Lexington Books, 1988).
8. John Cooley, op.cit., pp. 80-100.
9. Arthur J. Goldberg, "London's Libyan Embassy Shootout" in Benjamin Netanyahu's (ed.), *Terrorism: How the West Can Win* (New York: Farrar, 1986), p. 139.
10. Wiliam Gutteridge, *The New Terrorism* (London: Mansell, 1986), p.11.
11. Ibid., p.l5.
12. Paul Bremer III, "Counter-Terrorism Strategies and Progress", *Terrorism: An International Journal,* Vol.10 (New York, 1987), p.339.
13. John J. McCuen, *The Art of Counter-Revolutionary War* (London: Faber and Faber, 1966), p.129.
14. For details see Jan Tan Brink, *Robbespire and Red Terror* (London:

Hutchinson and Co. 1899).
15. D.M. Sehlagheck, *International Terrorism*, op.cit., p. 79.
16. Alexander Solzhenitsyn, *Gulaq Archipelago 1918-1956*, translated by Thomas P. Whiting (Collins: Fontana, 1976).
17. For details see, Augustus R. Norton and Martin H. Greenberg, *Studies in Nuclear Terrorism* (Boston: G.K.. Hall, 1979).
18. Jasjit Singh, Director, Institute for Defence Studies Analysis, New Delhi, in a personal interview.
19. Victor Ostrovcky and Claire Hoy, *By Way of Deception* (London: Arrow Books, 1991), passim.
20. K.J. Holsti, *International Politics* (New Delhi: Prentice Hall India Ltd., 1978), p. 275.
21. Bob Woodward, *Veil: The Secret Wars of CIA* (New York: Simon and Schuster, 1987), p. 27.
22. Young Hum Kin, *The CIA Problems of Secrecy in a Democracy* (Massachusetts: D.C. Health & Co., 1968), passim.
23. See Comually David Wise and Thomas B. Ross, *The Invisible Government* (London: Jonathan Cape, 1964).
24. Ibid., p.4.
25. *Indian Express* (Bombay), 18 December 1991, p.1.
26. Peter Wright and Paul Green Zgrass, *Spy Catcher* (New York: Viking, 1987), p.6.
27. Victor Ostrovsky, *By War of Deception*, op.cit.
28. Neil C. Livingstone and Terrell E. Arnold, *Fighting Back* (Massachusetts: D.C. Health and Co., 1984), pp.10-23.
29. Col.William D. Meale, "Terror, the Oldest Weapon in the Arsenal", *Army*, August, 1973, pp. 10-17.
30. "Patterns of Global Terrorisn", US Department of State Publication, 9862, Office of the Secretary of State, Office of the Co-ordination for Counter Terrorism, April, 1991, p.32.
31. Helmut Andics, *Rule of Terror*, translated by Alexander Lienen (London: Constable, 1969).
32. David Thompson, *Europe since Nepolean* (New York: Penguin Books, 1966), p.830.
33. D.M. Sehlagheck, *International Terrorism*, op.cit., p.81.
34. Paul Wilkinson, *Terrorism and Liberal State*, op.cit., p.38.
35. Alain Labrousse, *The Tupamaros* (Middlesex: Penguin Book, 1973).
36. Ibid.
37. The names of the agencies were censored.
38. Activities are censured from being published in the Press.
39. John S. Pustay, *Counter-Insurgency Warfare* (New York: The Free Press, 1965), p.163.
40. Allan E. Goodman, "Intelligence and Foreign Policy", *Current*, No.299, (January 1988), p.38.
41. *Congressional Digest*, Vol.67, No. 92, December 1988, p.289.
42. Walter Laquer, "Anatomy of Terrorism", in Frank Gregory and Joseph Palmer (Eds.), *Ten Years of Terrorism* by (New York: Crane Russak. 1979), p.12.

43. Frederick L. Schuman, *The Cold War: Restrospect and Prospect* (Lousiana: Lousiana State University Press, 1962), p.23.
44. Ibid., pp.80-86.
45. Paul G. Hoffman was the Head of International Co-operation Administration in New York in a Press Conference on 6th January 1949, qtd. in Ibid., p.23.

Chapter 4

Pakistan's Promotion of Terrorism in Punjab

A conceptual analysis is not enough unless it is supported by practical reality. Hence this chapter examines the case of Pakistan's use of terrorism in international relations with special reference to India. It highlights the case of Pakistan's use of terrorism to achieve its foreign policy goals in Punjab. The causes of the use of terrorism by Pakistan will be discussed at length in their historical perspectives.

It is relevant, to mention at the very onset that though nations get involved in both overt and covert use of terrorism, the case of Pakistan is that of overt rather than covert application. This chapter deals with Pakistan's foreign policy objectives in Punjab and the use of terrorism to achieve these goals.

Punjab, the land of five rivers has seen blood shed for one and a half decades. Thousands were killed during the 1980s and continue to be killed to date in sporadic acts of terrorism. During the 1990s the situation appeared to be totally under control. But what Punjab witnessed during the 1970s and 1980s cannot be written off. Table 1 gives details of violence and crime that took place in Punjab between 1980 and 1990. All these crimes were related to terrorism in some form or the other.

There are several reasons for this blood shed. But, one of the most significant reasons is Pakistan's support for militants fighting for secession of the state from India and the creation of an independent Sikh nation to be called Khalistan. Hence, this chapter examines the objectives of Pakistan's foreign policy goals in abetting terrorism in Punjab.

PAKISTAN AND PUNJAB: AN OVERVIEW

In the light of the fact that foreign policy is formulated on the basis of a nation's past experience, present requirements and future plans, it is relevant to highlight historical links between Punjab and

Pakistan. This historical analysis is important, because the political history of Pakistan is wedded with the history of Punjab. Evidently, the latter has an important contribution to the foreign policy of the former.

Table 1. Incidents of Cognizable Crime (IPC) Under Different Crime Heads in Punjab (1980-1990).

Year	Total Incidents Of Crime	Murder	Attempt To Murder	Kidnapping	Dacoity	TADA
1980	-	620	135	259	1	-
1981	13,588	555	133	279	1	-
1982	12,263	575	151	245	1	-
1983	13,960	-	169	204	9	-
1984	12,828	744	174	168	11	-
1985	11,185	646	142	164	10	-
1986	13,224	1,101	159	172	-	-
1987	15,017	1,388	137	182	157	-
1988	14,275	1,761	1,184	193	84	319
1989	14,166	1,667	1,171	243	37	248
1990	16,131	2,813	1,567	370	96	26

Source: Crime in India, National Crime Record Bureau, Vol. 1980 to 1990, (New Delhi).

The politics of border states in the Indian federation occupy an important position in the foreign policy-making of neighboring nations as their people share common social and political history. Therefore, Punjab, being the most serious victim in the creation of Pakistan happens to be an important factor in the foreign policy of Pakistan.

The relationship between Pakistan and Punjab goes back to the partition of Punjab in 1947. At that time the state was divided into East and West Punjab—between India and Pakistan respectively. A major territory of Punjab was awarded to Pakistan as per the Radcliff Award, which was introduced on August 18, 1947.[1]

On the basis of ethnic demography, the Muslim-dominated parts of the state were given away to Pakistan, while the non-Muslim (Hindus and Sikhs)-dominated territory remained with India. Thus, a major portion of Punjab became the main land of Pakistan. Lahore, the seat of the administration and economy of Punjab became part of Pakistan. This left most of the non-Muslim

Punjabi populace in bewildering state of affairs as their main source of livelihood was scrapped, and the riots and bloodshed that ensued the partition compelled them to migrate to India. While the Hindu Punjabis lost their commercial base, the Sikhs were the worst affected because besides losing economic resources, they lost the center of their religion. The holiest of all the Sikh religious shrines—Dera Baba Nanak Sahib—could not be included in the Indian Union despite the war cry of Master Tara Singh.[2] There were several other historical factors in the partition of Punjab which agitated the Sikh populace to a great extent. A brief history of Punjab would be useful to understand the Sikh psyche on Punjab and their link with present Pakistan.

A Short History of Punjab

The history of Punjab is best analyzed in the light of the history of Sikhs which practically begins with the organization of 'Khalsa' over three hundred years ago by Guru Gobind Singh—the tenth and the last Guru of Sikhism.

The objective behind the creation of 'Khalsa' was to build a force with the spirit of nationalism free from the social and religious evils of the time.[3] Its creation could also be analyzed in the light of the prevalent socio-politico-economic conditions during the time of Guru Gobind Singh Whose father, Guru Teg Bahadur Singh, was executed by Aurangazeb in 1675. The coercive policy of Aurangazeb created disillusionment and an opportunity for non-Muslims to organize themselves against the repression. Guru Gobind, who lost his father at the tender age of nine, grew up in that political atmosphere, and was the most suitable leader to fill the gap created by the assassination of his father. Inspired by the religious preaching of Guru Nanak and the call for militancy by Guru Hargobind (the Sixth Guru), he organized a militant force against Aurangazeb. Guru Hargobind was the first guru who emphasized the need for military adventure by bearing two swords—one as the symbol of spiritual power and the other as material power. But it was Guru Gobind who put the Sikh army on a regular footing.[4]

After the death of Guru Gobind, Guru Banda Singh (1708-1716) took over the domain of Khalsa Dal. He was the first to raise the slogan "Raj Karega Khalsa" (puritans will rule) in the political sense of the term.[5] He assumed power, captured Sarhind, issued coins in the name of the Guru and abolished the Zamindari system in Punjab.[6] By this time Sikhism had become a political force with religious fervor. The slogan "Raj Karega Khalsa," which originally meant the purification of the soul as a pre-condition to rule over people, got political recognition as the rule by Sikhs. Banda Singh emerged as the valiant warrior and laid the foundation of Khalsa Raj. He fought vigorously with two hostile forces to maintain a separate identity of the Sikh kingdom. On the one hand, he had to fight against the Moghals ruling over Delhi and on the other hand, he had to meet the challenges of Afghans in the Northwest frontiers. In the two frontal wars, his soldiers either died of starvation or became too weak to fight for want of food supply and other essentials. Ultimately, he was arrested and executed along with his army in Delhi on February 29, 1716.[7]

After the mass massacre and execution of Banda Singh, there was a temporary lull in the Sikh prowess. The Khalsa power could not bear the brunt of two hostile forces and there was internal squabbling filled with morose and tentative tranquility until 1721. Soon after, Mata Sundari, the widow of Guru Gobind, intervened and restored peace in Delhi and the Sikh leaders began to pour in Majha (now in Pakistan) for fresh action. This again brought the wrath of Moghals and they were put to severe torture and sufferings. However, administrations of both the Moghals and the Afghans were too weak to deter the spirit of the Khalsa at that time. They engaged themselves in building fortresses, increasing areas of influence and successfully befriended Adeena Beg, who was appointed as the Governor of Jallandhar by Ahmed Shah, the Afghan ruler of Lahore. Adeena Beg was a valiant warrior who further intensified the struggle of Sikhs against the Afghans. But his lust for power turned him against his Sikh ally and was ultimately killed after he ordered repression against the Sikhs.

The actual political power of Punjab did not come to Sikhs until the emergence of Maharaja Ranjit Singh who acceded to the throne of Lahore in 1799. With his shrewd political vision and secular attitude he brought all the squarely disseminated principalities of Punjab under one domain with due sanction from the Khalsa Panth. His kingdom expanded from Lahore to Jammu and Kashmir and he ruled for 50 years (1799-1849). It was during his regime that Punjab became a well-knit strong kingdom.

After his death in 1849, the fate of Punjab once again relapsed into darkness because Ranjit Singh did not leave behind a well-defined heir. He had many wives and so were the claimants for the throne. Tussles for power continued for some time and ultimately the Royal British Government, which had already made a mark in Punjab politics captured power from Maharaja Dalip Singh on March 29, 1849.[8]

Partition of Punjab and Creation of Pakistan

The brief historical background of Punjab gives an insight of relations between the Sikhs and the Muslims. The relations between the present Pakistan and Punjab should be seen in the light of these historical facts, which have left a far reaching impact on the local politics of Punjab and the regional politics of the Indian sub-continent.

The ethnic division of India in 1947 is one of the important factors that inspired the Sikh leaders to want to achieve sovereign status for Punjab as a Sikh state. However, this was too foreign an idea to be acceptable to the British government. The demography of the state did not show dominance of the Sikh populace in the entire region although they sat on the saddle of political power. The western parts of Punjab had the dominance of Muslims and the East too did not have a Sikh majority, which is explicitly clear from Table 2 of the following census figures of 1941.[9]

Table 2. Population of Punjab according to 1941 census

Religion	Percentage
Muslims	51
Hindus	35
Sikhs	12
Others	2
Total	100

The demographic figure did not support the idea of Sikh leaders. The ten British government declines to do any favor for them. But the representatives of the Sikh community were not prepared to accept this argument. As a matter of fact, underlying all the factors, the demand for a separate Sikh state has been one of the most significant issues for Sikhs in Punjab. The demand for Punjabi Suba during the 1960s or for Khalistan during the 1980s are off-shoots of the same urge. They had already tasted fruits of power in the past and were unwilling to compromise, specifically when the Muslims were granted Pakistan. Therefore, current political aspirations of the Sikh leaders should be analyzed in the light of their past experience.

Guru Hargobind sowed the seeds, Guru Gobind nurtured it and his successor, Banda Singh made the dream of Sikh political power a reality when he occupied the entire upper India and the Northwest Frontier Province and ruled over Punjab until the British government took over the throne from the minor child Prince Maharaja Daleep Singh.

At the time of the departure of the British colonial government, the same psyche hovered over the minds of the Sikh community. However, since the numbers of the Sikh population was not strong enough, the British government did not grant nationhood to Sikhs as they did to the Muslim league. The Marquees of Linlithgow in his personal letter clarified that the circumstances were not favorable for Sikhistan. He considered the claim for a Sikh autonomous state as far more preposterous than the claims of the Muslim League for Pakistan.[10]

With the partition of India, Punjab was divided into East and West. The western part, which went to Pakistan, was the main center of the Sikh polity. Pakistan exists today on reminiscences of Sikhism which Sikhs, living in India, Pakistan or American cannot forget. It is in this deep-rooted socio-economic and political environment that the relations of Sikhs with Punjab and Pakistan need to be understood.

During the pre-independence period, specifically when creation of Pakistan had become inevitable, veteran Sikh leaders were concerned about the fate of Punjab, which they did not want to part with, nor were they willing to let the whole of Punjab go to Pakistan. Their memory of the Sikh Kingdom was still fresh. The state of Punjab during the time of Maharaja Ranjit Singh was expanded as far as Peshawar (now in Pakistan) in the northwest, to Ladakh in the northeast, Montgomery in the south and Delhi in the east.[11] The same territorial boundary continued to exist within the periphery of Punjab until 1947. Thus for them, division was an option between the devil and the deep sea. They opted for the deep sea so that they could swim till they achieved an autonomous status for Punjab. It was under this influence that the Sikh Panth, led by Master Singh, adopted the resolution for division of Punjab in February 1946. The objective was to constitute a separate autonomous Sikh state within the Indian territory.[12] They were hopeful to achieve this goal because of Nehru's assurance, who clearly stated in the All India Congress Committee on July 7, 1946 that

> The brave Sikhs of Punjab are entitled to special consideration. I see nothing wrong in an area and a set up in the North wherein the Sikhs can experience the glow of freedom.[13]

So intense was their desire for a separate identity that even Jinnah tried to bargain with the Sikh leaders to avoid the division of Punjab. He had almost agreed to the formation of a Sikh state with military establishment of Pakistan.[14] But the Sikh leaders did not have confidence in Pakistan's military. Instead, they trusted the words of Nehru, which remained on paper.

The partition of Punjab, did not merely affect the political psyche of the Sikh community, the economy too was badly affected.[15] The majority of the Sikh population in Punjab were peasants. They were either feudal lords or rich farmers. As soon as the partition plan was implemented in 1947, their economy received a severe blow. They were compelled to abandon their land which was their main source of livelihood and prosperity. Even after the mass exodus from the west to the east, Sikhs did not have smooth sailing in settlement of disputes on transfer of property. Property left by the Muslims in Kapurthala district brought the two communities—Hindus and Sikhs—of Punjab at loggerheads. In the divided Indian side of Punjab, the majority belonged to Hindu communities until the state was reorganized in 1961. The Hindus had already occupied trade and commercial centers. Agriculture and petty business were the only sectors left for the Sikhs in the overall economy of Punjab.

The deteriorating economy was a matter of serous concern to the Sikh community, which holds wealth and prosperity in high esteem. Their enterprising zeal made them migrate far and wide to accumulate wealth rather than to remain in Punjab where there was a fewer concentration of industries. This mass exodus of Sikh populace from Punjab caused not merely demographic imbalance against the interests of the community,[16] but also affected the activities of the Panth which play an active role in the Sikh society.

Coupled with political aspirations and economic pressure, was anxiety over maintaining an identity in the Indian Punjab and an emotional attachment to religious shrines in Pakistan. While on one hand they had to struggle to maintain separate religious identity in India because they were obsessed with being contained in the greater Hindu fold of life, on the other hand, they were dissatisfied with the Radcliff Award, which placed the birthplace of Guru Nanak in Pakistan.

This complex history of Punjab has not only left an indelible mark on the polity of Sikhs, but has also influenced Pakistan's foreign policy in relation to India, specifically in Punjab. However, before examining the foreign policy objectives of Pakistan in Punjab, it is relevant to discuss political conditions that inspired Pakistan to intervene in Punjab.

POLITICAL UNREST IN PUNJAB: A CONDUCIVE ENVIRONMENT FOR EXTERNAL INTERFERENCE

The internal emergency imposed by the Indira Gandhi government in 1974 created a political environment conducive to internal conflict. The dismissal of a duly elected Akali government in 1980 brought utmost chaos in Punjab politics. The dictatorial rule and mass arrest of politicians under the Maintenance of Internal Security Act (MISA) brought an unprecedented hostile atmosphere in the body politic. Fundamental rights were suspended making even common people inimical towards the central government. Eminent leaders were arrested and people were compelled to be mute spectators of the Congress' tyranny during 1974-75.

Punjab, being a western border of India, is vulnerable to foreign aggression. The dictatorship of Indira Gandhi added fuel to the fire. The Pakistani intelligence hawks had been waiting for this kind of environment to bring about internal conflict on communal lines.

To make things worse, political development during the post-emergency period took a new turn that marked the beginning of mass political agitation in Punjab. The center of focus in the agitation was the Anandpur Sahib Resolution.

Anandpur Sahib Resolution

The Anandpur Sahib Resolution first adopted in 1973 at Anandpur

Sahib received mixed reaction in Punjab politics. The most controversial aspect of this resolution was use of the work "Sikh Quam".[17] This controversy was at the helm of the Punjab crisis. Innumerable interpretations of the resolution were offered causing much agitation. But no agreement could be reached as to which version was to be accepted. This disagreement was mainly because Indira Gandhi wanted to keep the issue alive for electoral gains.[18] The resolution thus became part of nation-wide controversy. It is important to highlight some of the issues raised later but whole controversial nature is sccpcd in the 1973 resolution.

There were altogether 12 resolutions adopted by the All India Akali Conference held at Ludhiana on October 28-29, 1973 under the administration of President Jathedar Jagdev Singh Talwandi.

The first resolution was of general political nature which demanded the decentralization of power so that Punjab could have full autonomy to maintain its cultural and linguistic identity. The second resolution called for the fulfillment of outstanding demands such as the transfer of Chandigarh to Punjab, the distribution of Ravi Beas Waters, and to increase the strength of Sikhs in the army. The third resolution was dedicated to economic guidelines for the state of Punjab as well as for India. Similarly, resolutions 4, 5, 6, 7 and 8 were also related to various grievances of the Sikh community against the central government.

However, the most controversial of all the resolutions was resolution number 9 that sought permission from the government of India to install a broadcasting station at the Golden Temple so that the Gurubani could fulfill the spiritual needs of Sikhs living abroad.[19] It was this resolution that received severe blows and was rejected outright. The Indian government had serious objections to this far- fetched demand. The term "Sikh Quam" or "Sikh Nationhood" as first introduced in 1973 had already brought the state of Punjab into political turmoil. Thus the further demand for a broadcasting station was enough for the Congress to brand the new demands as secessionist.

It is possible that if the government of India had given serious consideration to the other demands, the controversial portions of the resolution could have been dropped. But Indira Gandhi acted in most haste in rejecting the entire charter of the Anandpur Sahib resolutions. Some of the demands, as proposed in the resolutions were genuine and received enthusiastic support from the common people; for instance, greater autonomy in the governance of the state and decentralization of power. These were not merely genuine demands of Sikhs in Punjab, but also drew nation wide attention specifically in states ruled by opposition parties.

The outright denial of Akali demands opened a new chapter of confrontation in Punjab politics. It created such a commotion in the body politic of Punjab that the Akali Dal too was divided into two groups—the followers of a hardline approach and adherents to a softline approach.[20] The democrat stalwarts like Sant Longowal, Badal and Barnala were sidelined by the hardliners who were encouraged by the Congress to waken the Akali Dal. In the process of creating an instrument against Akali Dal, the Congress created a national problem.[21] The political bungling of the Congress ultimately inspired Pakistan to intervene. Pakistan intelligence was all out to shelter, train and protect misguided anti-Indian Sikhs abroad. On the occasion of the birth anniversary of Guru Nanak, November 8, 1984, thousands of Sikhs living abroad gathered at Nankana Sahib near Lahore. Important leaders among the participants were G.S. Dhillon and Jasbir Singh, brother of Bhindranwala who converted the religious congregation into a political meeting with the help of the Pakistan government.[22] The followers of the hardline approach were encouraged by the Pakistan intelligence agencies to support a violent revolution in Punjab. The following section highlights how the hardline Sikhs grew from an insignificant entity to a hero and from hero to martyrdom.

Emergence of Bhindranwale
Emergence of Bhindranwale in Punjab politics would be analyzed in the light of following three factors: (1) Political game plan of Indira Gandhi, (2) Inseparable link between religion and politics in Punjab and (3) Assistance from external forces.

Political Game of Indira Gandhi
The various interpretations of the Anandpur Sahib Resolution created a vacuum in the local politics of Punjab. Indira Gandhi, the Prime Minister, after having captured power at the general elections was determined to dismantle opposition governments of the states. Punjab fell under this category. The state government was under the leadership of the Akali Dal which was part of the

opposition alliance in 1977. In her fury to avenge the humiliating defeat of her party in the general elections, she ignored the geo-strategic significance of the state and the sensitive nature of Punjab politics. Politics in Punjab is not pure politics, but a combination of religious dictates of saints and politics of Sikh leaders. Therefore, the political destiny of the state of Punjab is determined by its political leaders who represent the 60 percent Sikh population of the state.

The politics of the Sikh masses is determined by Akali Dal which according to Sikh tradition, needs religious sanction to govern the state. But after the emergence of numerous splinter groups in the Akali Dal, religious sanction has lost its relevance. As a matter of fact all the local political parties in Punjab are named Akali Dal. The only difference is the prefix or suffix used.[23]

In so far as politics of the Akali Dal are concerned they have never been consistent. Being a regional party, its allegiances have been shifting from one party to another according to the prevalent situation and requirements of the state. So long as Congress dominated the political scene of the country, Akali Dal enjoyed patronage from Congress leaders. Indira Gandhi too had been supportive of Akali Dal until the proclamation of the emergency in 1974.[24] During the 1977 general elections, Congress did not file any candidate against Akali Dal, though Zail Singh did manipulate elections.[25] During this period, 1974 – 1977, there was a clear shift in the policy of the Akali Dal. When the 1977 general election was announced, the Akali Dal opted to join hands with oppositions to defeat Congress. This brought the wrath of Indira Gandhi against Akalis. In order to let down the Akalis, she encouraged Nirankari to dispel the influence of the former and capture the center stage of Punjab politics with the support of Congress. With this objective, she patronized Nirankari Baba Gurubachan Singh.[26]

It is believed that Nirankaris received financial aid from government secret funds.[27] Baba was purposely accorded VIP treatment wherever he went. The Ministry of External Affairs sent letters to its ambassador in Iran to welcome his when the latter was on a visit to Iran. The Iranian Sikhs protested and ultimately diplomatic privileges were withdrawn.[28] All these efforts were to portray the Baba as the real leader of the Sikh community. The Sikhs were totally averse to Nirankaris and specifically to Baba Gurubachan Singh who had hurled a volley of criticism against the

Sikhs in general and Akalis in particular. As a matter of fact, the Sikh community does not consider Nirankaris as followers of Sikhism. According to them Nirankaris are agents of Hinduism determined to tear the fabrics of Sikhism.[29] The idea of the Congress party for promoting Nirankaris as substitutes for Akalis further precipitated the anger of the Sikh religious leaders. The special honor accorded to Baba Gurubachan Singh within and outside the country by government agencies created a furor among leaders of the Sikh community. However, the event that brought landmark changes in Punjab politics was the Kanpur incident.[30]

Baba Gurubachan Singh and his followers, in collaboration with the Congress, organized a massive rally on September 25, 1978, in Kanpur. The Congress was determined to make the rally a success while other similar rallies, organized by the Nirankaris, throughout the country were foiled by the Akalis. The cooperation of the Congress caused anger of the Akalis. This resulted in violent clashes between the Akalis on the one hand and Nirankaris and the Congress on the other. This event was the turning point in the history of militancy in Punjab. The Akali leaders, specifically those inclined towards force and violence, resolved to venture into politics of violence and terrorism. The immediate outcome of this incident was the assassination of Baba Gurubachan Singh in 1980. The Baba and his 61 followers who were co-accused in the Amritsar carnage of Sikhs, i.e. on the baisakhi of 1978 were acquitted. The extremist Akali could not tolerate the injustice and killed the Baba.

The assassination of the Baba, proved to be an eye opener for Indira Gandhi. She realized that playing the Nirankari card against the Akalis could be counter-productive. First, because Punjab politics is not dominated by Nirankaris; and second, Nirankaris are not recognized as Sikhs. Thus, she renounced the idea of patronizing Nirankaris and left her son, Sanjay Gandhi and Zail Singh to explore someone within the Akalis who could influence Punjab politics in her favor. It was through the efforts of these two that Bhindranwale came into active Punjab politics.[31]

Meanwhile, the political agitation of the Akalis for greater autonomy continued. Several rounds of talks took place between the Central Government and the Akalis. But all these efforts were in vain. Scholars believe that the Central Government was interested in keeping the issues alive.[32] Indira Gandhi, as a matter of fact, showed utmost negligence to the causes when she selected the Foreign Minister, Narasimha Rao to negotiate with the Akalis to resolve an issue which was of pure domestic nature.[33] Demonstrating an extreme sense of indifference to Punjab problems she allowed her son Sanjay, a layman in politics, to intervene in the political affairs of the state. Sanjay picked up Bhindranwale from a remote village of Faridkot district of Punjab. Zail Singh and Sanjay Gandhi found in him a great personality and won his confidence. This alliance was the beginning of the Bhindranwale cult in Punjab politics.

In 1980, the Akali Dal was clearly dominated by moderates. But the ever-increasing influence of Bhindranwale gradually affected the psyche of the people. By 1982, Akalis were divided into moderates and extremists. The moderates allied with the opposition, and hance Congress extended its favor to the extremists. Sanjay Gandhi encouraged the extremists against the moderate Akalis.[34] Thus, the era of violence was ushered into Punjab politics.

While on the one hand, violent protest was encouraged indirectly by Pakistan on the other, India's Central government adopted a stern an humiliating course of action against the threat to disrupt the Asian Games in 1982. The following year, spates of laws were passed by the government of India in October after imposing President's rule on Punjab. The regulations such as— Punjab Disturbed Areas Act, 1983, Chandigarh Disturbed Areas Act, 1983, National Security (Amendment) Act, 1983, the Armed Forces (Punjab and Chandigarh) Special Powers Act, 1983, the Code of Criminal Procedure (Punjab Amendment) Act 1983, and Terrorist Affected Areas (Special Courts) Act, 1984—[35] further precipitated the situation. The implementation of these acts brought a sense of alienation on Sikh people from the mainstream of the nation. As a result, Bhindranwale drew the attention of Sikhs and acquired the status of a hero.

Inseparable Link of Religion With Politics
Inseparable link of religion with politics is another significant factor for the rise of Bhindranwale. The Sikh religious tradition demands sanction of Akal Takht to govern the state. The oft-quoted Punjabi proverb, "Raj Karega Khalsa," is the manifestation of this tradition. In this context, it needs to be reiterated that

Sikhism does not propagate the idea of separating politics from religion rather it says that politics or governance of the state is the temporal duty of religion. Guru Hargobind, the Fifth Guru of Sikhism, laid the foundation of the Akal Takht i.e. the seat of power and issued the Hukumnama (decree) for the followers. He, for the first time, hoisted the Sikh flag at Akal Takht in 1608.[36]

The foundation of the Akal Takht was to provide a political base for the Sikh community to enjoy freedom to be governed according to their own religious traditions. Ever since then Chief Khalsa Diwan and the elected representatives of the Sikh Gurudwara Prabhandak Committee (SGPC) spread throughout the country had been at the center of political power in Punjab. The priests and the representatives of the SGPC who also happen to be Sants in one form or another, have a far-reaching impact on the social and political life of the state of Punjab.

Therefore, the influence of religious leaders is inevitable in Punjab politics. The Sikh religious tradition preaches obedience to religious leaders. Guru Gobind, the last and the most important of all the ten Gurus in Sikhism gave clear instructions to his followers that the "Granth" and the "Panth," i.e. holy book and religious leaders are the only sources of guidance to the community. Hence, their psychological orientation is such that they follow the dictates of the Panth.[37] Every priest of Gurudwaras, scattered throughout the world, has considerable influence within the range of their domain. Their powers could be easily utilized to the extent of their area of influence. This is particularly relevant in the countryside where people pay blind obedience to religious leaders.

The emergence of Bhindranwale too could be attributed to this fact of socio-economic and political life of the people in the state. He drew popularity after assuming the priesthood of Damdami Taksal in 1977 and gathered strength from the Taksal which not only enjoys religious sanction but is one of the important religious institutions of Sikhism.[38]

Bhindranwale came to the Taksal for spiritual training under the guidance of the head priest, Kartar Singh Bhindranwale. He acquired spiritual knowledge from him and made his prowess felt at a very young age. His genuine desire for the advancement of the Sikh community and the aggressive style of functioning made him popular among the masses.[39]

Furthermore, indiscriminate humiliation and torture meted out to the Sikh Community on the eve of the 1982 Asian Games,[40] inspired more and more people to join his cadre. His spirit and valor influenced the people to such an extent that they started approaching him (Bhindranwale) than going to government agencies or courts to settle their disputes. The power given to him by the Damdami Taksal gradually emerged as the de facto power of the state.

Bhindranwale and his followers openly protested the moderate Akalis, and continued to attain popular support. Even Zail Singh approached him to fight against the Akalis in the SGPC. He gave him funds to fight the SGPC election.[41] His candidates, however, were routed. It was obvious that his next target was to capture the Akal Takht and ultimately, if the Congress does not come to the terms of the Anandpur Sahib Resolution to capture political power of Punjab by issuing a decree from the Akal Takht.

In the midst of these events, numerous changes took place. Bhindranwale rose to political power with the support of Sanjay Gandhi who died in 1982. His understanding with Indira and Rajiv was not strong enough to influence or to be influenced by each other. On the contrary, the gap between the two increased. Bhindranwale in an open interview made clear that if the Central Government does not give equal treatment to Sikhs, they have to give in to the demands of a Sikh state named Khalistan. He reiterated that Sikhs would not live in slavery. "I am neither for it nor against it," he said about an independent Sikh state.[42] The gap between the two gradually widened. The government of Pakistan aptly exploited this deteriorating political situation.

Assistance from External Forces

The 1974 recruitment policy of India's defense ministry and the indiscriminate humiliation during the 1982 Asian Games were turning points in the alienation of Sikhs from the mainstream of the country. Jagjivan Ram, the defense minister withdrew the special reservation for Sikhs in the recruitment to the military, which was in practice since British rule. Withdrawal of this old privilege irked the Sikh leadership to a great extent. Coupled with this was the uncompromising attitude of the Congress Party to resolve issues in the local politics of Punjab. This gave an impression to the Sikh populace that they government purposely let the situation pass to a dramatic climax to malign the image of the Sikhs as secessionist and at the same time to portray the Congress Party as enough to deal with any adverse situation.[43]

Pakistan had been taking stock of the situation and so had been eminent Sikh personalities abroad. While Pakistan supplied arms and ammunitions for the cause of Bhindranwale, the Non-Resident Indian (NRI) Sikhs provided funds and moral support.[44] Many of the militant organizations supported by Bhindranwale operated as conduits for assistance. They also influenced public opinion through distorted facts and figures against India,[45] which were propagated by Pakistani agents. Obviously, the government of Pakistan openly supported the idea of Khalistan. With the help of intelligence agencies Pakistani leaders assured full support for Bhindranwale and his associates and also provided infrastructure and facilities.

Continuous flow of arms and mercenary training was the most immediate need Bhindranwale and his followers had. Many of his followers were young school dropouts or unemployed youths wandering in search of jobs.[46] They were novices in the art and craft of militancy. However, providing training within the Indian territory was a difficult task. It was not possible to evade the roving eyes of the Indian intelligence. There was the possibility of being caught and punished by the Indian government. Hence, Pakistan came forward to offer safe havens for training young recruits. A number of training camps were set up in Lahore and Karachi where new recruits were trained under the command of Pakistani generals.[47] Once the training was over, they were sent back to Punjab for subversive activities.

Besides training facilities, Pakistan supplied weapons, ammunition and various telecommunication facilities to Bhindranwale and his associates. This aid by Pakistani leaders provided moral support and helped Bhindranwale's image expand to that of hero.[48] The lack of resources could have effectively arrested the rise of the Bhindranwale cult in Punjab but Pakistan leaders such as Zia would not allow to happen. Zia had already established good rapport with eminent Sikh personalities abroad. For example, he befriended G.S. Dhillon, a U.S. citizen and the president of Sri Nankana Sahib Foundation in Washington D.C. Dhillon's presidential duties included the management of Sikh shrines in Pakistan which brought the two in contact with each other. In their meetings, they did not merely discuss the management of Gurudwaras in Pakistan, but also the possibility of carving out a Sikh state from India.

Another disgruntled Sikh political leader who came into contact with Pakistani leaders (before General Zia came to power) in connection with autonomy for Punjab, was Jagjit Singh Chauhan who was Finance Minister in the Akali government for a short period before he escaped from India. This Sikh leader was invited by the Pakistan leader Zulfikar Bhutto to meet him in New York. In an interview he revealed that Bhutto and his delegates discussed the possibilities of a Sikh state. In the course of their discussions, Bhutto offered his cooperation to Chauhan in the following words:

> Sardarji, you have the keys of Nankana Sahib. Come there, we will help you and make it the capital of Khalistan. Start the movement from here.[49]

Inspired by this moral support, Chauhan placed a half page advertisement in the *New York Times* on October 13, 1971 giving a detailed explanation for the creation of Khalistan, an independent Sikh state.

Later, even after Bhutto was overthrown by Zia-ul-Huq, the relationship between NRI Sikhs with the Pakistani leaders did not receive any set back rather Zia chalked it out in a planned manner. General Zia found in Bhindranwale a good friend who could help him retaliate against the dismembering of Pakistan in the 1971 war that left Bangladesh an independent state.

These developments had a far-reaching impact on the Rambo personality of Bhindranwale. His furious speeches and style of functioning were applauded by Sikh leaders abroad, while his plan of action was covertly implemented and supported by the government of Pakistan. The support included the provision of infrastructure facilities to help create the state of Khalistan. Through his followers, Bhindranwale maintained links with Pakistani agents and Sikh leaders abroad.

Thus, these controversial personalities from the NRI Sikh community, in collaboration with Pakistan government, encouraged Bhindranwale to emerge as a hero. This dimension will be further explained later when discussing the role of the Panthic Committee.

On the basis of the above description, it can be argued that the prevalent political conditions in Punjab were conducive for

Pakistan to intervene in the affairs of the state. However, before examining Pakistan's promotion of terrorism in Punjab, it is equally important to understand foreign policy objectives of Pakistan in Punjab—to analyze what Pakistan intends to gain by abetting terrorism in India.

Thus, the subsequent part of the study highlights foreign policy goals of Pakistan in Punjab.

PAKISTAN'S FOREIGN POLICY GOALS IN PUNJAB

Various issues are involved in Pakistan's foreign policy towards India. The issues range from political, to economic, to religious, to defense and to regional considerations. All these issues played a significant role in foreign policy making of Pakistan. However, the predominant factor in Pakistan's foreign policy towards India is the liberation of Bangladesh in 1971. It brought a new dimension to Pakistan's foreign policy objectives towards India, specifically as far as Punjab is concerned.

Bangladesh War: A Factor

The 1971 war for the independence of Bangladesh from Pakistan was the turning point in Indo-Pak relations. India's active participation in the guerrilla war by the Mukti Bahini against Pakistan's government changed the entire gamut of relations between the two countries.

India's involvement in East Pakistan was one of the most controversial issues in international politics during the 1970s. India could not convince the world community that her intervention in East Bengal had moral justification nor could Pakistan deny the atrocities and injustices committed against the Bengali populace. But one thing was quite obvious—the entire international community stood as one against India's intervention in East Bengal.

It is a fact that India played an important role in the Bangladesh affair. So vivid was India's involvement in the liberation of Bangladesh, that the First Secretary of the Indian Deputy High Commission in Dakka, P.M. Ojha, was expelled by the Pakistan government. He was charged with having links with anti-Pakistan elements and for abetting a secessionist movement in East Bengal. These facts were revealed in the Agartala conspiracy case.[50] The Pakistan government could not accept the fact that creation of Pakistan in 1947 had already invited further division in the Indian sub-continent. The growth of divisive forces was clearly written on the walls of Pakistani politics. India's active support for Bangladesh served as an alchemist.

East-West Divide

Ever since the creation of Pakistan, the political leaders of East and West Pakistan were at loggers head. This divide was inevitable.

Jinnah made his first post-independence visit to Dakka in March 1948. It is worth noting that when he declared, at Dakka University, that Urdu would be the only state language of Pakistan, there was such a commotion in the convocation hall that he had to leave without completing the speech.[51] This cultural and linguistic divide, however was not of much significance until the assassination of Liaquat Ali Khan in October 1951.

The Bengali leader, Khwaja Nazimuddin who served as the governor General from 1948 to 1951, never felt comfortable with Yahya sitting one the saddle of the armed forces. Yahya, being a western educated Punjabi did not favor Nazimuddin. Because of dominance of the Punjabis (60 percent of the total) in the army, which is sacrosanct to politicians, Nazimuddin could take charge of power only after the death of Liaquat Ali. However, since the Bengalis were more active than the Punjabis, Sindhis or Pathans in the politics of Pakistan, the former had a clear edge over the latter's in the National Assembly. But, in sheer disregard to these political realities, Punjabis were reluctant to induct Bengalis in to power. In spite of having won the first general election, the Awami League was denied the right to form a government in Pakistan.

Table 3. Successive Rulers of Pakistan 1951-1958

Name of the ruler	Cultural and Linguistic Identity	Tenure
Khwaja Nazimuddin	Bengali	1951-1953
Md. Ali Bogra	Punjabi	1953-1954
Gen. Ghulam Md. (Democratic Institutions suspended)	NWFP	1954-1955
Md. Ali Choudhary	Punjabi	1955-1956
H.S. Suhrawardy	Bengali	1956-1957
I.I. Chandrigar	Bengali	1957-1957Oct-Nov
Feroz Khan Noon	Punjabi	1957-1958

Table 3 highlights the tussle for power between the Bengalis and the Punjabis in Pakistan during 1951-1958. The confrontation between the two, as a matter of fact, caused the militarization of politics and the emergence of Bangladesh in 1971.

Table 4. Economic disparities between East and West Pakistan

	East Pakistan	West Pakistan
Areas in Sq. Miles	54,501	301,236
Population (1970)	70 million	60 million
Five Year Plan Allocations:		
1st Plan	32 %	68 %
2nd Plan	32 %	68 %
3rd Plan	36 %	64 %
4th Plan	52.5%	47.5%
Foreign Aid Allocations:	20-30%	70-80%
Export Earnings	50-70%	30-50%
Import Expenditure	25-30%	70-75%
Jobs and Services:		
Civil Services	16-20%	80-84%
Military Jobs	10%	90%

Foreign Trade (in Rupees):	East Pakistan		West Pakistan	
Years	Exports	Imports	Exports	Imports
1947-52	4,581,596	2,128,628	3,785,806	4,768,923
1952-57	3,969,766	2,159,552	3,440,371	5,105,093
1957-62	5,508,335	3,831,924	2,724,169	8,554,170
1962-67	6,922,694	7,063,692	5,754,368	15,960,025

The gap between the two gradually became wide. None of them were willing to compromise. Had the Bengali leaders been allowed to assume power in East Pakistan without unnecessary interference, it is possible that the territorial integrity of Pakistan would have been maintained. It is amazing that East Pakistan witnessed a procession of eight Governors within four years before the final revolution for Bangladesh took place.[52]

Furthermore, economic disparity between the communities also contributed to the upheavals in Bangladesh. Table 4[53] highlights discrimination between West and East Pakistan.

These economic factors culminated in Martial Law Regulation No. 60 which came into force on December 21, 1969. The enactment of this regulation brought all the political activities to a halt under the pretext of security measures. This the divide between the two got further widened. At this stage, East Bengal politics were at a point of no return. Thus, Indian involvement only gave a decisive direction to the obvious political aspirations of the Bengali population of Pakistan.

Coupled with psychological alienation and economic disparity were other political developments in Pakistan. After the Tashkent Declaration, signed between India and Pakistan in 1966, the internal politics of Pakistan were precarious. Ayub Khan had to step down and power handed over to Commander Yahya Khan in March 1969. Khan is discredited for having ruled Pakistan more mercilessly than any previous ruler though he deserves some credit for conducting the first general election of Pakistan in December 1970.[54]

The result of the election did not favor the Punjabi-dominated military junta or the Pakistan's People Party (PPP). People voted for Awami League which was based in East Bengal. The military junta declined to handover power to Sheikh Mujibur Rehman, the leader of Awami League. This reluctance of the ruling Pakistani military regime created further complications in an already turbulent political atmosphere.

It was this precarious situation that gave India an opportunity to intervene in East Pakistan. The Pakistan government further soured its relations with India when in January 1971 Bhutto accorded VIP treatment to hijackers of an Indian Airlines Fokker Friendship plane. The government of Pakistan allowed the hijackers to blow the plane within the protected area of the Lahore International Airport.[55] Further crack down on the Bangladesh movement in Dakka by the Martial Law Administration of General Tikka Khan, gave a new dimension to the problems between India and Pakistan. The coercive policy towards the Bengali population not only agitated the Bengali masses but it also posed a refugee problem for India. Thousands of Bengalis crossed over to the Indian territory out of fear and intimidation, and many of them flocked to the liberation movement called Mukti Bahini which indulged in subversive activities against the Pakistan government.

India seized this opportunity and provided all possible assistance to the Mukti Bahini, the climax of which was the Indo-Pak war in Decemeber 1971 and subsequent creation of Bangladesh as an independent sovereign state. Until India joined hands with the Bengali population, Mukti Bahini was a volunteer force without any direction. It was only with the cooperation of India that volunteers were trained in guerilla warfare against the government of Pakistan. Thousands of them were recruited for training in subversion.[56] It is clear that without Indian support Bangladesh would have remained a distant dream.

FOREIGN POLICY OBJECTIVES IN PUNJAB

After the liberation of Bangladesh, Pakistan's foreign policy took vindictive turn towards India though publicly it pretended to be friendly by signing the Shimla Agreement in July 1972. The turn of events gradually affected the political scenario in Punjab. The question that begs an answer is: What does Pakistan intend to achieve in Punjab? There are three major foreign policy objectives of Pakistan in Punjab.

1. Creation of a separate Sikh state
2. To discredit India's secular credentials, and
3. Fragmentation of India.

Creation of a Separate Sikh State

One of the significant objectives of Pakistan's foreign policy in Punjab is to carve out a pro-Pakistan separate Sikh state from the Indian side of Punjab. Pakistan's foreign policy makers intend to avenge the loss of East Pakistan in the 1971 war by creating Khalistan.

The defeat in the 1971 war caused fear psychosis in Pakistan of being contained by India. Clearly Pakistani leaders were reluctant to accept India's hegemony in the region. In spite of being aware that India is a bigger power with significant military (fourth largest in the world), economic and technological resources,[57] Pakistan wants to claim equality with India. This psyche was prevalent right from the beginning. It further intensified after the 1971 war. Vendetta got so deeply rooted that Pakistani leaders adopted an eye for an eye approach to wards India. Avenging the 1971 war became the most evident objective of Pakistan toward India.[58]

This objective could be accomplished by fueling the cessation of either Jammu and Kashmir or Punjab. These two are the only bordering states prone to secessionism.[59] It is important to point out here that Pakistan's objective in Jammu and Kashmir is not the creation of a separate and independent state but to grab these from

India. Hence, Punjab is the only state that could serve this cessation that Pakistan yearns for. In order to achieve this goal, Pakistan has adopted certain strategies. These are (a) alienation of Sikh masses from within through propaganda, and (b) external support for the cause of their grievances against the government of India.

The first strategy, obviously, is to alienate Sikh community from the mainstream of India's socio-economic and political life. Without mass alienation of the local population Pakistan would not be in a position to achieve its goal. The government of Pakistan employs various propaganda measures to flare up suppressed feelings of Sikh masses including those serving in the Indian army. The ISI agents unleashed a series of hostile propaganda messages highlighting the 1982 humiliation of Sikhs and the action of the Indian army at the Golden Temple. The propaganda said Sikhism and its holy places were in danger under the repressive regime of Hindu India.

Such propaganda has a far-reaching impact on Sikh sentiments. It affected them to such an extent that some of the Sikh army personnel deserted the Indian army and marched towards Delhi and Punjab to protect the Golden Temple.[60] Operation Blue Star had immensely damaged the sentiments of Sikh masses. People were in anguish and alienated as planned by Pakistan. The local Punjab politics were in turmoil. There was neither strong leadership nor any political direction. The Akali politics, too, were in shambles. Coupled with political turmoil was the political design of Indira Gandhi, which further precipitated the situation. Gandhi's dismissal of the Badal government in 1979 and her support for Bhindranwale against the Akalis caused severe damage to the fabric of Punjab politics.[61] The political situation gradually deteriorated from bad to worse from 1980 onwards. It was the kind of situation Pakistan had been aspiring for since the creation of Bangladesh. Pakistani leaders found the situation favorable to strike in Punjab. The psychological alienation had already taken place. Now it was time for Pakistan to provide external support to create a pro-Pakistan Sikh state. In a well-planed strategy, Pakistan government under the leadership of Zia-ul-Huq, launched state-sponsored terrorism in Punjab to help create Khalistan.[62]

General Zia and Jagjit Singh Chauhan, the self-proclaimed and exiled leader of the proposed state of Khalistan, became very close friends. When Chauhan visited Pakistan as a pilgrim, the government of Pakistan accorded him special treatment; and helped him to organize a massive rally of Sikhs which was attended by several aspirants of Khalistan from the U.S. and Canada.[63] In fact, his pilgrimage to Pakistan turned into a political opportunity for Pakistan to malign India's image. To strengthen the movement for Khalistan, as proposed by Chauhan, the Zia Sikh youths. A place called Kasur, 15 kilometers from Eminabad in Gujranwala district became the principal center for training.[64] Zia-ul-Huq deliberately increased the number of Sikh pilgrims visiting Pakistan and deputed intelligence and other enforcement agency staff to maintain direct contact with them so that they could be inducted to the separatist movement.[65]

Innumerable school dropouts and unemployed youths from Punjab were lured into this profession due to lack of money and career prospects.[66] Sikhism preaches that active life leads to prosperity. The unemployed youths could not sit idle. The teachings of Guru Nanak emphasized the value of life in the following lines *Nam Japo, Kirat Karo and Band Chako*, i.e. recite the name of god, perform duties and enjoy fruits of your deeds. This is the basic teaching of Sikhism. But the lack of job opportunity and constant political instability in the state forced young Sikhs to just roam around. As a result, the youth of Punjab became prone to exploitation by Pakistan.

The rise of Bhindranwale and the fortification of the Golden Temple by militants in 1984 made it evident that Pakistan provided all kinds of assistance to aspirants of Khalistan. The KGB, the Soviet intelligence agency, intercepted a conversation between CIA agents and some Pakistani officials which said that some of the Khalistanis planned to proclaim a Khalistan state from the premises of the Golden Temple of June 4, 1984.[67] It is obvious that Pakistan, in connivance with militants, was all set to create a separate Sikh state. Lt. Col. Sher Nawaz of the Pakistan military disguised himself as Captain Amrik Singh of the Khalistan Commando Force (KCF) and entered Golden Temple two days before Operation Blue Star took place. He got the feel of the Indian forces around the temple but managed to escape the night before the operation began because he did not want to be a prisoner in India once again. He was a Captain and POW during the 1971 war. He could not forget the humiliating defeat of Pakistani forces by India and was determined to take revenge. But once again he had to be disappointed and escaped to Pakistan.[68]

Discredit India's Secular Credentials

Another significant objective of Pakistan is to discredit India's secular credentials.

Pakistan was created on the basis of ethnic demography and religion whereas India opted for secularism. This ideological divide made India more popular compared to Pakistan in world politics. But it was hard for Pakistan to accept that India was a secular state.[69] Pakistani leaders branded India as a repressive Hindu regime rather than a secular state. They aspired to tarnish the tolerant image of India.

This objective of Pakistan could be achieved by creating a communal rift in Jammu and Kashmir and Punjab. Both these states of India are minority dominated. Punjab, however, is better placed to waken India's secularism because Sikhism as a religion is recognized as an offshoot of Hinduism. By alienating the Sikh masses, Pakistan intends to emphasize the Hindu India is more communal as it does not allow Sikhism, an offshoot of Hinduism to exist as a separate religion. In support of this argument, the Hindu Code bill is often targeted as a deliberate attempt to discredit Sikhism as a religion. It is imperative to note that the Hindu Code bill recognizes Sikhism as a sect of Hinduism.[70] This interpretation is denounced by the Sikh leaders. They do not accept that Sikhism is a Sect of Hinduism. According to them, Sikhism is a separate religion and must be treated as such. They abhor any idea of being contained in the broader Hindu fold of life.[71] Any effort by Hindu religious institutions to undermine Sikhism causes anguish in the Sikh community. They have been aggressive about their religious belief and this psyche is exploited by Pakistan to gain political mileage.

Secularism or religious tolerance is not a novel concept in India. Hinduism, the main religion of India, is not a religion in the same sense as Christianity and Islam. These two religions are organized missions while Hinduism is diversified and has no fixed ideology as such. Historians rightly define Hinduism as gradual evolution of thought and philosophy.[72] In the six systems of Indian philosophy,[73] one can often come across contradictions. These contradictions in Hinduism make it a tolerant religion. In other words, it has tremendous scope for assimilation.

Pakistani leaders are aware of this fact and find it difficult to change this identity unless they adopt a definite strategy to tear the fabric of communal harmony. This is achieved by adopting propaganda techniques in different phases.

The first phase was propaganda for mass agitation against the government of India so that it could not gain confidence of the people. The sentiments of people were outraged and encouraged to rebel through mass media. The political errors committed in the state by the Congress government were highlighted and taken out of proportion and people made to believe that the government of India was dominated by Hindu chauvinists. The Pakistani propaganda repeatedly emphasized that human rights of minority communities in India are not well protected and the Sikhs are being discriminated against. "Hate India" propaganda was widely disseminated through mass media like newspapers, radio, television, videotapes and through rumors, direct contacts and intelligence agencies. Well-concocted news articles, columns and pamphlets were disseminated to the Sikh masses.[74] Documented films and videotapes were released to highlight alleged atrocities committed by Indian state authorities. The incidents of violence and crime that often take place in Punjab, were reported and highlighted in the government controlled radio and television media of Pakistan as the outcome of state terrorism in India.[75] These incidents were given communal gloss to instill a sense of insecurity among the Sikhs.

This propaganda strategy of Pakistan proved quite effective. People, were swayed by the communal propaganda unleashed after Operation Blue Star. The demand for Khalistan, which was a vision of a few disgruntled Sikh personalities like Jagjit Singh Chauhan, Sohan Singh, Baldev Singh and their associates, now became a cause of common concern. People were brainwashed by heinous propaganda, the outcome of which was mass exodus of Sikhs from India during the early 1980s. A good number of them migrated to Canada, the U.S., Britain and other European countries. They carried and shared their bitter experience meted out to them during the course of political turmoil in Punjab from 19800-1984. Within India itself, there was a mass exodus of Sikhs from other states to Punjab. A feeling was created that Punjab would secede from India.[76]

The point of concern, however, is what does Pakistan intend

to gain by discrediting India's secular credentials? One gain is quite obvious and that is that by doing so, Pakistan does not have to seek secularism for herself. It definitely brings ego satisfaction to say that, India is as communal or theocratic as Pakistan happens to be. But this is too small a factor to be incorporated into a foreign policy agenda.

Secularism as such has no relevance in political relations between the two countries. But, it does affect the regional environment of the Indian sub-continent where both India and Pakistan are important players.

Secularism is the backbone of the pluralistic society of India. It is true that the majority population of India belongs to the Hindu fold of life. However, since the advent of Islam in the Indian sub-continent, not only has the ancient Hindu way of life been influenced by Islam in the northern provinces of India, but a sizeable population is now converted to Islam. Therefore, any aberration in India's secularism instantly affects peace and harmony of the Indian society. Communal riots and hatred are common symptoms of the disease India suffers from whenever there is deviation from its secular credential.

By fomenting communal disharmony, Pakistan aims to divide Indian society on religious lines and to create conflict from within.[77] Constant internal conflicts would affect politico-economic conditions and would weaken the political and moral will of India. Thus, a destabilized Punjab is in the interest of Pakistan because it would debilitate India's strength in South Asia, and give Pakistan a chance to counter-challenge India's strong hold in the region. In other words, by destabilizing Punjab, Pakistan could be the beneficiary in a regional race for power.

Fragmentation of India

The western boundary of India is of major concern to Pakistan. Punjab and Jammu and Kashmir are the adjoining states sharing a common boundary with India and Pakistan.

Jammu and Kashmir is divided into three divisions. Jammu, Kashmir and Ladakh. But it is only in the valley of Kashmir that Pakistan can stake a claim. Ladakh is dominated by Buddhists who favor India. Similarly in the Jammu division, the population ratio between the Muslims and the non-Muslims is considerably low and favors non-Muslims. However, this part of the state is of strategic significance as it is the immediate neighbor of Pakistan and is equally dominated by the Sikhs and the Hindus. In order to capture the entire state, the Pakistani military has to cross the Akhnoor border, i.e. in the Jammu division where they cannot expect blind obedience from the people. This region has a sizeable population of the Sikh community. Therefore, any incidents that take place in Punjab, explicitly or implicitly affect the political environment of Jammu also. Thus, this demographic and strategic condition of the Indo-Pak western frontier suits Pakistan's desire to create disturbance and foster the fragmentation of India.

Despite the fact that Pakistani leaders are conscious of the reality the creation of a Khalistan state would be detrimental to their own existence, their hatred for India is so acute that they tend to make wrong calculations.[78] Their policy in Punjab is an example of the same miscalculation. Jammu and Kashmir and Punjab are the immediate targets of Pakistan. Pakistani leaders assume that cessation of either of the two states would be tentamount disintegration of India.

This objective of Pakistan directly affects external and internal security aspects of India. As a matter of fact the support for the creation of a separate Sikh state and the efforts to discredit India's secular credentials are offshoots of Pakistan's objective, which is to weaken India's military strength.

The defense capability of India is the most important issue in the Indo-Pak rivalry. Pakistan's foreign policy is dominated by the urge to strengthen defense capability vis-à-vis India. Pakistani leaders react hysterically to any suggestion that undermines Pakistan's status in comparison to India.[79] This was the driving force behind all the defense treaties Pakistan has signed so far. The supply of weapons continues to flow from the U.S. and international markets, and a lion's share of the budget is allocated to defense expenditure. However, despite accumulation of sophisticated weapons from the West. Pakistan could not disintegrate India. The Indo-Pak war of 1965 already proved that Pakistan is not in a position to do so. Pakistani military had almost reached Srinagar and was ready to capture Jammu and Kashmir.[80] But due to a brilliant strategy by the Indian army—to open a new front in the Lahore section—the Pakistani army had to retreat in spite of the huge stockpile of arms and sophisticated weapons they had received from the West. Hence, war as an action to disintegrate

India did not and cannot help Pakistan to achieve its goal.

Thus, the only means left to weaken India is fueling internal conflicts and poising external threats from across the border. Pakistani policy makers had visualized this option well in advance, but it only took shape during the regime of Zia-ul-Huq.[81]

By bringing about disharmony in Punjab, Pakistan's sole objective is to destabilize India. In other words, leaders in Pakistan aspire for the fragmentation of India from within. Riots, violence, and internal upheavals would keep the armed forces engaged in maintaining law and order within the state.[82] As a result the strength of forces at the border would gradually reduce making the western border vulnerable to Pakistani forces.

Punjab has been vulnerable to external threat form time immemorial. Political turmoil in Punjab therefore causes instability in the nation. For example, political agitation in Punjab during the 1980s brought the entire nation under siege. Normal social, economic and political life remained paralyzed in India for more than a decade, bringing the nation's progress to a near halt. Its impact was felt as far as the northeastern states of India. It was also during this period that Assam agitation reached its zenith, internal violence and conflict flared up and the country did appear to be breaking into pieces. Though Punjab is relatively peaceful at the time of this writing, because of the stern administrative action taken by the KPS Gill and law enforcement agencies, people too have realized the woes of terrorism. Still the government of India cannot take the present lull as permanent peace. The present divide in Akali politics might spark agitation in Punjab any time and Pakistan would again attempt to use terrorism. It would be pre-mature to conceive that the police administered peace in Punjab has lessened the hidden danger of the secessionist movement. Pakistan could again try to revive terrorism in Punjab with the help of the Afghan Mujahideen and Akali dissidents.[83] Therefore the Government of India needs to keep a tight vigilance in Punjab.

TERRORISM: PAKISTAN'S SOLE WEAPON IN PUNJAB

Before analyzing the nature of Pak-sponsored terrorism in Punjab, it is important to highlight the advantage to Pakistan if Khalistan were to come into existence.

Creation of a friendly Khalistan is of strategic importance to Pakistan. Pakistan's foreign policy analysts always perceive India as a threat.[84] They believe that the security of the India sub-continent is divisible and can be shared equality between India and Pakistan—Pakistan in the northwest and India in the northeast.[85] Therefore, creation of Khalistan on the northwest border would achieve this objective, and eliminate the perceived threat from India. Scholars in Pakistan believe that the non-existence of a barrier on the Indo-Pak border is a dangerous situation for the security of Pakistan.[86] Khalistan as a buffer state would provide this barrier, and ensure territorial integrity. Also, carving out Khalistan would cut Jammu and Kashmir from Indian roadways and railways and help Pakistan to capture and break Jammu and Kashmir from India in the same way that Bangladesh was broken from Pakistan.

Politically, the creation of Khalistan could bring stability in domestic politics of Pakistan. It would boost the morale of the political leadership and exalt Pakistan's status in the region to that which is at par with India. This would help the Pakistan government deal firmly with secessionist movement in Sindh and Baluchistan.

Also, a friendly Khalistan would serve economic purposes. The prospect for trade and commerce for Pakistan would increase. Pakistan has not yet opened commerce and trade with India for fear of being contained by India.[87] The prospect for economic gain would increase if Khalistan were created. The ancient trade route via Lahore and Amritsar would be again open for trading in Punjab and Jammu and Kashmir. The land route from Lahore and Amritsar, which was closed for trade after the partition in 1947, directly connects Srinagar with Pakistan.

These are the three major advantages for Pakistan if Khalistan were to come into being. It is difficult, however, to fathom how genuine Pakistan's aspiration for a separate Sikh states is. There are some in Pakistan who believe that if a separate Sikh state came into existence, sooner or later, it would claim some territory of Pakistan also,[88] which would threaten the territorial integrity of Pakistan. The hypothesis, though based on historical realities, is far-fetched and is unlikely to be reckoned with in the near future. It would influence foreign policy of Pakistan only when Khalistan comes to exist. Hence, this aspect is not highlighted in the present study.

NATURE AND INFRASTRUCTURE OF PAK-SPONSORED TERRORISM IN PUNJAB

The goals of Pakistan's foreign policy in Punjab differ from those of Jammu and Kashmir. Apparently the nature of Pak-sponsored terrorism too differs from what which is practiced in Jammu and Kashmir. While exploitation of religious sentiments is the most dominant factor in Jammu and Kashmir, Punjab being a non-Muslim dominated state has a different equation in Pakistan's foreign policy.

Religious propaganda would not be that effective in Punjab as in Jammu and Kashmir. The major territory of Punjab dominated by a Muslim population was already acceded to Pakistan in 1947 against the wishes of Sikhs who desired a United Punjab. As a result, Sikhs and Muslims are not in good terms, nor do they enjoy the confidence of each other. The government of Pakistan is fully conscious of the fact that the Radcliff Award of 1947, which allocated Dera Baba Sahib (the holiest of all the Sikh Shrines) to Pakistan, is deeply resented by the Sikh community. Pakistan, apparently, would not like to take a risk which might be counter productive to its territorial integrity. Therefore they have adopted a path of calculated risk in abetting terrorism in Punjab.

The objective of Pak-sponsored terrorism in Punjab is simply cessation of the state from India as accession to Pakistan was ruled out way back in 1947 when the representatives of the Sikh community gave their verdict in favor of India.[89] Since India did not have major political problems during the early post-independence period, Pakistan did not adopt unlawful methods for cessation of the state. The bitter experience of partition was still fresh in the minds of the people and there was hardly any opportunity for the Pakistan government to intervene in domestic politics of Punjab. Unlike Jammu and Kashmir, where Pakistan government used almost all the instruments of foreign policy to capture the State, Punjab was placed in a different agenda. It was clear to policy makers that while East Punjab could not be part of a Union of Pakistan, it could be utilized to achieve one of their foreign policy objectives in India, i.e. to promote secessionism. This objective of Pakistan could be achieved only by sponsoring terrorism in Punjab with the help of the local population.

Operation Tupac was the code name given by Indian defense analysts to Pakistan's plan of subversion in India. To be fair, it must be mentioned that there is no full evidence to prove or disprove that the Zia government adopted or implemented Operation Tupac or any such plan of action. But his action in

Punjab and Jammu and Kashmir during the 1980s and that he was inspired by the story of Amaru,[90] the Chief of Pampamarca in Peru who in the eighteenth century, fought against the Spanish colonization of Uruguay affirms the widely held belief that Zia was behind Pak-sponsored terrorism in India. Although Operation Tupac was more directed towards Jammu and Kashmir than to Punjab, it had direct implications on terrorism in Punjab because the infrastructure provided to Jammu and Kashmir militants was also made available to Sikh militants. In fact, rhetorical support to Sikh militants served a double purpose for Pakistan. On the one hand, the government created dissension and law and order problems for India, and on the other, raised funds for its ordinance factory by selling arms to the militants. It is intriguing to note that Sikh militants were encouraged to buy arms and ammunitions whereas the Jammu and Kashmir militants were not only supported but also funded.[91]

These differences in the nature of Pak-sponsored terrorism in Punjab from that in Jammu and Kashmir was related to the different objectives of Pakistan. For example, one other objective of the Pakistan government is to tarnish India's international image and sway world opinion. Now, it needs to be noted that when there is a change in objective, the modus operandi or the implementation of the plan also changes. Therefore, a close examination of the nature of Pak sponsored terrorism in Punjab reveals three phases each related to the intended objective at the time.

The first phase in the nature of Pak-sponsored terrorism in Punjab was alienation of the Sikh population from the main stream of India so as to fuel the movement for a separate Sikh state named Khalistan. The second phase was marked by subversion of the state machinery and mass agitation against the government so as to create political instability in Punjab. Finally, the third phase was characterized by a reign of terror in Punjab. People became victims of violence and counter-violence from the militants and the administration respectively. In this phase the infrastructure provided to Sikh militants by Pakistan was in the form of intelligence agencies and the Pak-based Panthnic Committee.

Intelligence Agencies

The contribution of Pakistan's intelligence agencies in abetting terrorism in Jammu and Kashmir will be discussed at length in the next chapter. The differences in the operations of intelligence agencies in Punjab from those in Jammu and Kashmir are related to geographical location. All the units of Pakistan intelligence agencies such as ISI and FIU active in Jammu and Kashmir also operate in Punjab. While ISI functions in connivance with the Pakistan-based Panthic Committee, the FIU members operate at the borders between India and Pakistan.

In Punjab, the ISI has two major tasks. First, the government of Pakistan has carved out a separate cell in ISI to provide infrastructure for Punjab terrorists. Its major task is to formulate policy in consultation with the Panthic Committee and other militant outfits such as the Khalistan Commando Force. Bhindranwale's Tiger Force, Khalistan Liberation Force and Babbar Khalsa. All these four terrorists groups receive policy direction from ISI.[92]

The second but very important task allotted to the ISI in Punjab is to exercise control over militant activities. This is critical in Punjab (as opposed to Jammu and Kashmir) because Pakistani intelligence hs to deal with non-Muslim outfits and cannot expect blind obedience from Sikh militants. Thus a certain amount of restraint is essential, especially in the light of the fact that many Sikhs aspire to see the Punjab of Maharaja Ranjit Singh. Hence ISI is empowered to monitor the activities of Sikh militants.[93]

Panthic Committee

The contribution of ISI and other intelligence agencies would not be of much significance without the active participation of the Pak-based Panthic Committee as far as terrorism in Punjab is concerned.

Panth and politics go together in the social and political life of Punjab. Because of the religious interference in politics—which is the way of social life in Punjab—the Panthic Committee has a lot of power. The dictates of the committee are observed as divine order and are followed by the people.

The Panthic Committee consists of five members elected from amongst the religious heads of Akal Takht of Amritsar, Anandpur Sahib, Damdama Sahib, Patna Sahib and Nanded. They are collectively called Panth or the upholders of the Sikh religious faith. But the situation in Pakistan is different. There is too much politics in the Panthic Committee, and many political sub-groups have emerged out of it. In Pakistan, there are altogether three Panthic Committees. The first is led by Paramjit Singh Panjwar, the second by the Sohan Singh Jafarwal and the third under the control of another Sohan Singh. These groups are more involved in politics than in maintaining religious order. By virtue of being members of the Panthic Committee, they have access to the resources and manpower of Gurudwaras that they then exploit for extra religious activities in Pakistan.

In 1925, the Gurudwara Act was passed which made Shiromani Gurudwara Prabhandhak Committee (SGPC) the custodian of all Sikh religious shrines along with their enormous resources.[94] The SGPC also functions under the dictates of the Panth. The Panthic Committee uses these enormous resources of money, manpower and infrastructure for its own gain. The SGPC is thereby empowered to take care of the management of Gurudwaras, while the Panthic Committee takes care of decision-making.

In India, the Panthic Committee and the SGPC, which is dominated by Akalis, can influence politics and policies of both the central and the state governments, because Punjab which is dominated by Sikhs (60 percent of the total population) is of strategic significance to the national security and territorial integrity of all of India.

But in Pakistan, the scenario is different. The Sikhs are an extreme minority and the Panthic Committee has no right to intervene in governance or politics of the state. Sikhs have no choice but to observe their faith and remain at the mercy of the government. This is one of the important factors that give the Pakistan government an opportunity to influence and to utilize the services of the Panthic Committee to achieve its foreign policy goals in Punjab. During religious gatherings in Gurudwaras for the celebration of birthdays and martyrdoms of Sikh Gurus, the Pakistani intelligence agencies exercise influence on the ideology and social behavior of the religious heads and through them influence the common people.[95]

In conclusion, the role of the Pak-based Panthic Committee[96] in abetting terrorism in Punjab should be analyzed and understood at two levels.

First, the Panthic Committee serves as coordination with the ISI in Pakistan's policy formulation sponsoring of terrorism in

Punjab. Pakistani terrorist and destabilization policies are made in consultation with the Panthic Committee to win their confidence and receive their cooperation in the execution of the plans. But, in reality, this consultation is more a formal gesture than a genuine desire by the Pakistani government to cooperate.

Pak-sponsored terrorists use premises of the Gurudwaras as hideouts or shelter before or after acts of subversion. It has been revealed by police findings that terrorists coming from Punjab to Mumbai or any other parts of India are usually harbored in different Gurudwaras of the cities.[97] Their family members are well looked after by the Committee so that militants can indulge in violent acts without any fear for security for their family members. Within the Gurudwaras, terrorists and their family members are provided with medical facilities, food and all their essential requirements.

There is also evidence that the Gurudwaras in Pakistan are also used for hoarding arms and ammunitions which in due course are moved to different Gurudwaras in India disguised as food and other essentials required to maintain Gurudwaras. The huge stockpile of arms recovered from the Golden Temple in the 1984 Operation Blue Star is a manifestation of this fact. All these murky transactions are conducted and coordinated by the Pak-based Panthic Committee.

Secondly, Panthic Committee plays an important role in propagating hatred and violence against the government of India in Punjab. The members of the Panthic Committee have direct interaction with the people who revere and obey their religious leaders. This religious status is emotionally exploited by the members of the Panthic Committee. By delivering speeches charged with religious sentiments and by revealing certain incidents of torture meted out on the Sikh community in the early 1980s (during the Punjab agitation) the Pak-based Panthic Committee instigates people to take arms against the government of India. The end result was that thousands of young Sikhs were mobilized in the name of an imaginary autonomous Sikh state to turn to terrorism the outcome of which was violence, counter-violence and bloodshed for decades.

This chapter has made it clear that all the violence, political instability and the radical calls for secession from India and the creation of an autonomous Sikh state called Khalistan are a direct result of Pakistan's use of terrorism as an instrument of its foreign policy objectives in Punjab.

REFERENCES

1. Kirpal Singh, *The Partition of Punjab* (Patiala: Punjab Unviersity Press, 1972), pp. 7-37.
2. Khuswant Singh, *A History of the Sikhs* Vol.II, (Delhi: Oxford University Press, 1977), pp. 298-301.
3. Teja Singh and Ganda Singh, *A Short History of the Sikhs 1469-1765*, Vol.i, (Bombay: Orient Longman, 1950), p.72.
4. Khuswant Singh, *A History of the Sikhs*, Vol.I, op.cit., p.98.
5. A.C. Banerjee, *The Khalsa Raj*, (New Delhi: Abhinav Publication, 1985), p.32.
6. Teja Singha and Ganda Singh, *A Short History of the Sikhs*, op.cit., p.80.
7. Joseph Davey Cunningham, *A History of the Sikh* (London: John Murray, 1849), p.95.
8. Ibid., pp. 92-95.
9. *Census of India*, 1941, Punjab, Vol.VI, (Shimla: Government of India Press, 1941).
10. Marquess of Linlithgow, Private and Personal Letters MSS.EUR.F. 125/11 (New Delhi : Viceroy's House, 1942).
11. Satinder Singh, *Khalistan: An Academic Analysis* (New Delhi: Amar Publication, 1982), p.82.
12. Gurmit Singh, *History of Sikh Struggles*, Vol.1, 1946-66 (New Delhi: Atlantic Publications, 1989), p.49.
13. *The Statesman* (Calcutta), 7 July 1946.
14. Maharaja Yadvinder Singh of Patialla, *The Tribune* (Ambala), 19 July 1959.
15. Paul Wallace and Surendra Chopra, *Political Dynamics of Punjab* (Amritsar: Gurunanak Deo University, 1981), p.120.
16. M.J.. Akbar, *The Siege Within* (Middlesex: Pengiun Books, 1985), p.170.
17. *White Paper on Punjab Agitation*, (New Delhi: Government of India, 10 July 19840, pp. 67-167.
18. Patwant Singh and Harji Malik, *Punjab: The Fatal Calculation* (New Delhi: Patwant Singh, 1985), p.39.
19. *White Paper on Punjab Agitation*, op.cit.
20. Paul Wallace and Surendra Chopra, *Political Dynamics of Punjab*, op.cit., pp. 43-46.
21. Rajinder Puri, "What Its All About" in Amrik Singh, *Punjab in Indian Politics*, op.cit., p.56.
22. V.B. Kilkarni, *Pakistan: Its Origin and Relations with India* (New Delhi: Sterling Publishers Pvt.Ltd., 1988), pp.2748, XXX.
23. Some examples are: Akali Dal (Longowal), Akali Dal (Barnala), Akali Dal (Tohra), Akali Dal (Badal), Akali Dal (Man) and Stri Akali Dal.
24. M.J.. Akbar, *The Siege Within*, op.cit., p.189.
25. *The Telegraph* (Calcutta), 22 December, 1983.
26. Jagjit Singh, *The Sikh Revolution* (New Delhi: Bahri Publications, 1981), pp.47-53.

27. Gurmit Singh, *Sikh Struggle*, Vol.II, op.cit., p.57.
28. Ibid., p.26
29. Sri Ram Sharma, *Punjab in Ferment* (New Delhi: S. Chand & Co. 1971), passim.
30. Gurmit Singh, *Sikh Struggle*, Vol.II, op.cit., pp.52-3.
31. Armik Singh, *Punjab in Indian Politics*, op.cit., p.6.
32. Harcharan Singh Baine in Amrik Singh's *Punjab in Indian Politics*, op.cit., p.138.
33. Ibid.
34. Patwant Singh and Harjit Malik, *Punjab: The Fatal Calculation*, op.cit., p.41.
35. *The Sikh Review*, Vol.xxxiii, No. 379, July 1985, p.48.
36. Gurmit Singh, *A History of Sikh Struggle*, Vol.I, op.cit., p.25.
37. Gobinder Singh, *Religion and Politics in Punjab* (New Delhi: Deep and Deep 1986), pp. 47-127.
38. The Taksal is the centre of religious preaching. The training for recitation of the Granth is mainly imparted in the Taksal itself. It is a religious training centre for youths.
39. Gopal Singh, *A History of the Sikh People* (New Delhi: World Book Centre, 1979), p. 739.
40. Amrik Singh, *Punjab in Indian Politics*, op.cit., p.16.
41. Kuldip Nayar and Khuswant Singh, *Tragedy of Punjab: Operation Bluestar and After* (New Delhi: Vision Books), 1984, p.24.
42. *Surya India* (New Delhi) 16-12-1983, pp. 13-6.
43. Patwant Singh, *Fatal Calculation*, op.cit., p.41.
44. White Paper on Punjab Agitation, op.cit., p.19.
45. Ibid.
46. Satyapal Dang, *Genesis of Terrorism: An Analytical Study of Punjab* (New Delhi: Patriot Publishers 1988), pp.32-38.
47. Kuldip Nayar and Khuswant Singh, *Tragedy of Punjab*, op.cit., p.133.
48. Gopal Singh, *A History of Sikh People*, op.cit., p.739.
49. *India Today*, 15 December 1993.
50. Jyoti Sen Gupta, *History of Freedom Movement in Bangladesh* (Calcutta: Naya Prakashan, 1974), pp.193-198.
51. S.M. Burk, *Pakistan Foreign Policy* (London: Oxford University Press,1973), p.398.
52. Ibid.
53. Tariq Ali, *Can Pakistan Survive* (Middlesex: Penguin Books, 1983), p.87.
54. Herbert Fieldman, *The End and the Beginning of Pakistan 1969-74* (London: Oxford University Press, 1975), p. 49.
55. For details see, Jamna Das Akhtar, *Pak Espionage in India* (Delhi: Oriental Publishers, 1971), pp. 35-45.
56. Lachchman Singh, *Indian Swords Strikes in East Pakistan* (New Delhi: Vikas Publishing, 1979), p.14.
57. K. Subramanyan, *Indian Security Perspectives* (New Delhi: ABS Publishing House, 1982), p.167.
58. Jagjit Singh Chauhan in an interview to *India Today*, 15 December

1993, p.65.

59. After the creation of Bangladesh, Pakistan has lost its accessibility to North Eastern states of India where there has been tendency of secessionism. For details see B.G. Vergese, *An End to Confrontation* (New Delhi: S. Chand., 1972), pp.65-71.

60. K.V. Krishnarao, *Prepare or Perish: Study of National Security* (New Delhi : Lacer International, 1991), p.297.

61. Satyapal Dang, *Genesis of Terrorism*, op.cit.

62. V.D. Chopra, R.K.. Mishra and Nirmal Singh, *Agony of Punjab* (New Delhi: Patriot Publishers, 1984), pp.95-101.

63. V.B. Kulkarni, *Pakistan: Its Origin and Relation with India*, p.xxx. 4. op.cit., p.XXVII.

65. J.N. Dixit, *Anatomy of Flawed Inheritance Indo-Pak Relations, 1970-94.* (Delhi: Konark Publication, 1995) p. 51.

66. Gurmit Singh, *History of Sikhs*, Vol.3, op.cit., p.1 and *Punjab Kesri*, 29 October, 1984.

67. B. Sarkar, *Pakistan Seeks Revenge and God Saves India* (New Delhi: Batra Books, 1997), pp. 31-40.

68. H.S. Gour, *The Hindu Code*, (Nagpur), p. 201.

69. Khuswant Singh, *History of Sikhs*, Vol.II, Op.cit., p.213.

70. Romila Thapar, *A History of India* (Delhi: Penguin Books, 1966), p.131.

71. See S. Radhakrisdhnan, *Indian Philosophy* (London: George Allen and Union, 1923).

72. Afsir Karim, *Counter Terrorism: The Pakistan Factor*, op.cit., p.150-52.

73. Ibid.

74. M.J. Akbar, *The Siege Within*, op.cit., p.200.

75. Kulkarni, *Pakistan*, op.cit., p.243.

76. Tariq Ali, *Can Pakistan Survuive?*, op.cit., p.124.

77. Keith Collard, *Pakistan's Foreign Policy* (Hong Kong: Hong Kong University Press, 1959), p.6.

78. Ibid.

79. Jagmohan, *My Frozen Turbulence in Kashmir* (New Delhi: Allied Publishers, 1991), p.408.

80. Afsir Karim, *Counter Terrorism*, op.cit., p.14.

81. *Sunday Observer* (Bombay), 27 November 1994, p.1.

82. *South Asian Studies*, Vol.12, No. 182, Jan-June and Jul-Dec. 1977, p.51.

83. Stephen P. Cohen, *The Security of South Asia* (New Delhi: Vistar Publications, 1987), p.232.

84. Aslam Siddiqui, Pakistan Seeks Security (Pakistan : Longmans Green & Co., 1960), p.16.

85. Leo E. Rose, "India's Regional Policy" in, Stephen P. Cohen, op.cit., p.8.

86. Satinder Singh, *Khalistan*, op.cit., p. 153.

87. Alain Labrousse, *The Tupamaros* (Middlesex: Penguin Book, 1973, p.15.

88. Gurmit Singh, *A History of Sikh Struggle*, op.cit., p.94.

89. *Indian Express* (Bombay), 12 June 1992.

90. Afsir Karim, *Counter Terrorism*, op.cit., p.48.
91. Ibid., p.48.
92. Office of the Director General of Police, Intelligence, Punjab, Monthly Terrorist Review on Punjab, Copy No.22, Secret (Chandigarh: May 1993), p.37.
93. Ibid.
94. Kapur, *The Punjab Crisis*, op.cit., p.23.
95. Office of the Director General of Police, Monthly Terrorist Review on Punjab, pp. 30-35.
96. First Panthic Committee for the cause of Khalistan was set up in Amritsar on 26 January 1986 under the leadership of Sohan Singh who went to Pakistan latter. *Sunday Observer*, 10-16 February 1991, p.5.
97. *Times of India* (Bombay), 6 March 1992.

Chapter 5

Pakistan's Use of Terrorism in Jammu and Kashmir

The previous chapter argued that Pakistan's foreign policy objective is to create an independent friendly Sikh state between India and Pakistan. However, the same cannot be said of Pakistan's foreign policy goal in Jammu and Kashmir. This chapter illuminates Pakistan's foreign policy objectives in Jammu and Kashmir and shows how terrorism is used to achieve them.

THE KASHMIR TANGLE

Kashmir, the land of abundant natural beauty, is the major bone of contention between India and Pakistan. It does not need to be reiterated that India considers Jammu and Kashmir an integral part of the Union, while for Pakistan, it is disputed territory. India's claim is based on historical reality. [1] Srinagar, the capital city of the state, was founded by the great Mourya King, Ashonka, who ruled the valley during the third century BC. [2] Ever since then, Kashmir has been governed by kings and queens of India belonging to different religious faiths.

But Pakistani leaders reject this historical position. Their understanding of the history of Kashmir only goes as far back as the medieval period, when the majority of Kashmiri Hindus, who believed in monism, i.e. Shivaism, converted to Islam. To the contrary, India's position on the history of Kashmir goes back to the beginning of civilization in Kashmir. India, being secular in character, cannot interpret history in terms of religion. Pakistan's claim for Jammu and Kashmir is also based on the principle of ethnic demography laid down by the Mountbatten Plan for the partition of the Indian sub-continent. The Mountbatten Plan prescribed that the Muslim-dominated provinces constitute the dominion of Pakistan. It was decided that there would be two dominions in the sub-continent and all princely states had to accede to either of the two. But the British government was impatient to transfer power. Instead of transferring power to the two dominions, the imperial government simultaneously transferred the power to innumerable princely states.[3]

This complicated the situation. The Maharaja of Kashmir opted for an independent status rather than accede to either of the two dominions. He signed a Stand Still Agreement with Pakistan and sent the same proposal to India. Unlike Pakistan, the government of India kept the Kashmir affairs in abeyance. Pakistan, on the other hand, was impatient to integrate Jammu and Kashmir. Jinnah was suspicious of Maharaja Hari Singh's integrity and could not trust him. This distrust undermined his political wisdom and judgment. Despite having signed the Stand Still Agreement with the maharaja, Jinnah imposed economic sanctions on Jammu and Kashmir to exert pressure on him to secede from India. This strategy was not just counter productive but fatal for Pakistan's own interest in the state. It was this action of the Pakistan government that brought India's active involvement in the affairs of the state.

Economic Sanctions, Aggressions and Accession
The partition of India left Kashmir solely dependent on the Pakistan cities of Lahore and Karachi for business transactions. This is because the state was not well connected either by roadways or railways with the rest of India. This made Kashmir dependent on Pakistan for all essential requirements, like food grains, kerosene, gas, and other commodities. This was the most vital reason why Maharaja signed an immediate Stand Still Agreement with Pakistan. The agreement clearly maintained that Pakistan would continue supplying essential commodities to the state.[4]

However, by August 1947—in sheer violation of the agreement—the Pakistan government halted the supply of essential commodities to Kashmir on the pretext that transportation was not available. But sufficient transport was suddenly available to carry invaders from the North-West Frontier Province (NWFP) to attack Kashmir on October 22, 1947.[5] This inhuman and coercive attitude of Pakistan towards Kashmir affected adversely the administration of the state government. The following lines of the telegram from the Prime Minister H.C. Kak of Kashmir addressed to the Governor General of Pakistan bears the testimony of the prevailing situation in the State:

Ever since August 15, 1947 in spite of agreement to observe Stand Still Agreement, increasing difficulties had been felt not only with regard to supplies of petrol, oil, food, salt, sugar and cloth from West Punjab, but also in the working of the postal systems which have been most detrimental. Savings bank accounts refused to be operated. Postal certificates were not cashed, and checks were not honored by branches of West Punjab.[6]

The situation further worsened when on October 22, 1947, Pakistan launched an armed attack on Kashmir and penetrated the state up to Baramulla, in the vicinity of Srinagar.[7] Forces of the Maharaja were not in a position to repel Pakistani aggression, which was in the form of guerilla warfare. The attackers indulged in looting, arson and plundering of Kashmir. The Maharaja negotiated with the Pakistani authorities through envoys and gave their assurances of a peaceful accession to avoid incursion. This fact was revealed later by a prominent member of the National Conference, M. Sadiq, who confessed that shortly before the invasion, the party deputed him to Pakistan government to respect the right to self-determination of Kashmir's people and to abide by their sovereign will on the question of accession to either India or Pakistan. But he found it of no use as Pakistani leaders were unwilling to let the Kashmir issue be decided by a referendum.[8] In sheer disregard for the Maharaja's overtures the Pakistan army along with NWFP fighters launched the armed attack to seize Kashmir by force.

The first tribal force that numbered 2,000 passed through Abbottabad in trucks fully equipped with arms and ammunition which could not have come from the limited means of tribal factories and workshops. Most of the war equipment was supplied through Pakistan's Muslim League Offices. A separate call, known as Kashmir Fund, was set up to meet the expenditures for the invasion.[9] Kurshid Ahmad, a senior aid to Jinnah had been deputed to supervise the situation, but was captured by the Indian army at Srinagar, and sent back to Pakistan.[10]

It was under these circumstances that the Maharaja of Jammu and Kashmir, in confidence with the National Conference leader, Sheikh Abdullah, sought assistance from India. It is important to note here that the accession of Kashmir to India was not a pre-condition for the rescue operation in Kashmir at the crucial hour. India did not ask the Maharaja to accede to India,[11] in fact until the major raids began, India had made no move towards Kashmir.[12]

So India was asked to help while Jammu and Kashmir were an independent state. However, Lord Mountbatten, the first Governor-General of free India, was against the dispatch of Indian troops to Kashmir unless it became a part of the Indian Union. This issue was discussed at a high level Defense Committee meeting in Delhi. The Maharaja was represented by Sheikh Abdullah in the meeting. At the end of the meeting it was decided that Jammu and Kashmir had to accede to India if Indian troops were to protect the state from further plunder and pillage. The outcome of this discussion was the accession of Jammu and Kashmir to India on October 26, 1947.

Thus, the state, with an 80 percent Muslim population, acceded to India causing immense harm to Pakistan's credibility as the champion of Muslims in South Asia. The issue became more humiliating for Pakistan when local people welcomed the decision of Sheikh Abdullah as it was ensured in the Instrument of Accession that a people's mandate would be ascertained as soon as the situation became normal. Pakistan, however, never accepted the validity of Kashmir's accession to India. On the contrary, it made Kashmir a major factor in its foreign policy vis-à-vis India.

PAKISTAN'S FOREIGN POLICY GOAL IN JAMMU AND KASHMIR
Ever since the accession, the Kashmir issue has dominated Pakistani politics. Kashmir has become a constant source of friction between India and Pakistan. The Kashmir issue also affects the internal politics of Pakistan.

Pakistan's foreign policy toward India comprises of several combinations of objectives.[13] For example the objectives in Rajasthan and Gujarat are economic but in Punjab and Assam they are political. However, as far as Jammu and Kashmir are concerned, Pakistan's sole objective is territorial expansion. Put simply, Pakistan wants to acquire the state from India.

The acquisition of Jammu and Kashmir is a top priority in Pakistan's foreign policy agenda in its relations with India. Pakistani leaders are categorical that no bilateral negotiation with India will bear fruit unless the Kashmir issue is settled. The leaders rightly observe that underlying all other political developments in Pakistan is the problem of its relations with India particularly the unresolved issue of Kashmir. It has not only dominated the agenda of Pakistan's foreign policy, but also that of the defense, economy and domestic politics of the country. [14] This preoccupation with India by Pakistani politicians is deeply rooted, first, in their perceived threat from India, and second, in the humiliating accession of Jammu and Kashmir to India, which undermine their credentials for creating an Islamic nation in the Indian sub-continent. Bhutto himself admitted that the principal challenge to Pakistan comes from India. [15]

The challenges, as perceived by Pakistan are (a) to maintain territorial integrity and (b) India's effort to undermine Pakistan as an Islamic state. The first obsession was most evident during the 1950s. It is true that in the beginning Indian leaders did not want to compromise and agree to the partition of India. But after the creation of Bangladesh, the question of territorial challenge to Pakistan did not arise. After the Bangladesh war, Indira Gandhi made it clear that Pakistan was a reality and there is no rationale for Pakistani leaders to think in terms of territorial threat from India. [16] This clear stand by India towards Pakistan's territorial integrity makes it obvious that the self-conceived challenge to their territorial integrity is a hoax which Pakistani leaders have nurtured right from the time of the partition and use to bolster their own political fortunes.

The other hypothetical challenge from India could be that of an ideological threat to Pakistan as an Islamic state. Unlike Pakistan, India, a predominantly Hindu society, is a secular nation. But Pakistan finds it hard to believe that millions of Muslims live Islamic lives in Hindu India. [17] The co-existence of Hindus and Muslims erodes the logic for the creation of Pakistan as a haven for Muslims. This secular system of India poses a challenge to Pakistan as a nation. To put it precisely, Indian secularism is perceived as a threat by theocratic Pakistan.

The accession of Jammu and Kashmir to India and the rise of Bangladesh further precipitated this obsession of Pakistan. Within 25 years of Pakistan's creation, the country had disintegrated, and another homeland for Muslims of South Asia come into being in 1971. The incident was a blow to Pakistan's ideological convictions about its own existence. It created an identity crisis for Pakistan. [18] Leaders were let down by the turn of these events, but did not lose hope. They reestablished themselves firmly and looked towards Jammu and Kashmir to compensate the loss of Bangladesh. Therefore, while the acquisition of Kashmir has been their objective since the beginning, the creation of Bangladesh strengthened it. There is a feeling that conquest of Kashmir could help Pakistan overcome its weaknesses as a nation.

Gaining control over Kashmir could empower Pakistan in many ways. First, it would enable Pakistan to regain the lost confidence of the Muslim population in this region. Soon after the partition, Pakistan lost the confidence of the Muslim population. Muslims who migrated from India did not receive equal treatment; they were treated as second-class citizens in Pakistani society. And by 1971 the most populated state (East Bengal) had led the movement for the creation of a separate Pakistan. So disillusioned were Muslims with the new political system of Pakistan that an eminent leader lamented that the partition was a mistake, collective madness and a death wish Muslims of the sub-continent.[19] These were initial setbacks for Pakistan as a nation, which political leaders in Pakistan tried to compensate for by rallying people around the Kashmir issue. If Pakistan succeeds in acquiring Jammu and Kashmir from India the leaders could claim to be the upholder of Islam in this region. While in this point, it is important to reiterate that Pakistan wants to attain leadership of Islamic countries. This objective can only be achieved if it enjoys the confidence of the Muslim population in this region. Victory over Kashmir could boost Pakistan's image in the Muslim world and increase its chances of becoming the leader of Islamic states in South Asia.

Second, conquest of Jammu and Kashmir would strengthen Pakistan's desire for setting up an autocratic state in the garb of Islam. Since the creation of Pakistan, political leaders have assured their people that a democratic republican system would be set up. But nothing concrete and lasting has come in practical reality until now. Instead, the military has emerged as dominant in the political system. Military dictatorships prevailed over and any democracy experiments. The pre-dominance of the military is justified by both the military rulers and the civilian leadership because it protects interests of Pakistan in Kashmir, and also because of the incompetence of civilian governments.[20] The Kashmir problem is therefore used as a shield to impose military rule and as a sword to settle domestic political problems. In the name of Islam both the military and the civilian government want to impose Sharia rule though the elites and the educated classes don't approve of it.

Third, Pakistan has been constantly engaged in internal conflicts and squables. Conquest of Jammu and Kashmir would be a morale booster for the solution of to solve domestic problems in Sindh and Baluchistan. It could provide succor to maintain territorial integrity of the country.

Finally, once Jammu and Kashmir accedes to Pakistan, the country would be in a position to search for a political ideology for the nation. An ideology based on culture, civilization and socio-economic conditions is a vital factor for a nation to go in certain well-defined path. Because of various factors that lead to the creation of Pakistan, the country is deprived of a national ethos which comes from a well-defined ideology. Mingling religion with ideology spoils the meaning of both terms. An ideology could be dismissed if it proves not viable. The disintegration of the Soviet Union is an example of the rejection of communist ideology. But the same cannot be applicable to religion.[21] Pakistani leaders have used religion itself as the ideology. However, intellectuals in Pakistan, disapprove of this idea. They would rather establish a political ideology for the nation than mix it with religion. They believe that unless Pakistan adopts a political ideology based on socio-economic conditions, it will be difficult for the country to survive as a modern nation-state.[22]

The search for an ideology, however, cannot be achieved as long as Kashmir is not integrated to Pakistan, because politics of Islam is the only game Pakistan can play to acquire Kashmir. When the Kashmir tangle is settled once and for all, Pakistani leaders can give thought to national ethos and come up with a political ideology for the nation. These are compulsions that encourage Pakistan to desire to conquer Jammu and Kashmir.

CLASH OF OBJECTIVES

Before analyzing various instruments used by Pakistan to conquer Jammu and Kashmir, it could be said that Pakistan's foreign policy clashes with the aspirations of the Kashmiri people.

Pakistan government portrays itself as sympathizer for their Kashmiri brethren. But, as a matter of fact there is there is clash of objectives between the government of Pakistan and the aspirations of local people in Kashmir.

Jammu and Kashmir Liberation Front (JKLF) is the main group fighting for the liberation of the state. However, they have made it clear that independence is their ultimate goal. They neither want to be part of India nor of Pakistan, and are determined to maintain their own identity.[23] It is because of this position that the government of Pakistan has lost interest in JKLF. The Pakistan government, with the support of Kashmiri militants in Pak-occupied Kashmir (PoK), organized cleavages within the JKLF. They have successfully created separated groups that toe the Pakistani line of approach. Hizb-ul-Muhideen, Ikwane Muslimeen, and Allah Tiger, Harkat-ul-Ansar, etc. are among those splinter groups that support assension to Pakistan. These groups receive overwhelming support from the Pakistani government while the JKLF bears the brunt of officials and intelligence agencies of Pakistan. These facts came into light in Operation Vikram, the counter-terrorism operation mounted by the Indian Army during the 1980s. The successful anti-militancy campaign in northern Kashmir revealed that there is a growing rift between Kashmiri terrorist groups and their supporters in Pakistan.[24] The pro-Pakistan, Hizb-ul-Mujahideen, for instance, accused JKLF of being in league with the Indian government. It alleged and claimed to have evidence to prove that the JKLF is responsible for killing of Hizb-ul-Mujahideen members in the valley.[25] Its leader Amanullah Khan, accused the government of Pakistan of trying to ban JKLF by declaring it a terrorist group.[26] Further, in an interview, he clarified that the Nawaz Sharief government accused him of being a terrorist because JKLF did not toe their ideological line.[27]

The bitterness in the relationship between the two foes of India is mainly because JKLF aims for independence whereas Pakistan's thrust is to annex the state. The Pakistan government has no consideration for independence of Kashmir, though some Pakistan goals such as that of do sometimes Sharief refer to independence for Kashmir as a third option.[28] But, these haphazard statements do not have any reasoning. They are just a move by Nawaz Sharief and others to restrain defiance within the JKLF ranks. The government of Pakistan and JKLF were at loggers-heads when the security forces of Pakistan clashed with the latter in the first week of February 1992. Ten people were killed in the clash and there was pressure on Nawaz Sharief to resolve this problem. It was under this situation that Nawaz Sharief floated the idea of third option. Otherwise, there is no agenda in Pakistan politics that can guarantee independence to Jammu and Kashmir.

It is obvious that Pakistan's only foreign policy objective in Jammu and Kashmir is territorial, i.e. to acquire the state from India. The following section, thus, highlights Pakistan's efforts in the past to conquer the state through conventional means.

EFFORTS TO CONQUER JAMMU AND KASHMIR THROUGH CONVENTIONAL MEANS

Pakistan has used all acceptable foreign policy investments to conquer Jammu and Kashmir. These are as follows 1) through political process, 2) through warfare, 3) through the UN, 4) through diplomacy and propaganda, and 5) through foreign aids.

Political Process

The political process for accession of Jammu and Kashmir to Pakistan started as soon as the British government transferred power to the two dominions.

Jinnah sent delegates to Srinagar to woo the Maharaja for peaceful accession of Jammu and Kashmir to Pakistan. One of the most prominent among the delegates was Major Shah, the secretary of military affairs to Jinnah. Jinnah sent Shah to convince the Maharaja that his status and privileges would be maintained and assured that the Maharaja should not be alarmed by the emergence of the National Conference of Sheikh Abdullah.[29]

Thus, the political negotiations began way back in 1947 itself, which resulted in the Stand Still Agreement between the government of Pakistan and the Maharaja of Jammu and Kashmir. The Maharaja also gave assurance to the leaders of Pakistan that the fate of the Kashmir would be decided only after ascertaining the will of the people as agreed upon by the two signatories. So long as this is not done, the state will not accede to either of the dominions. These efforts by Pakistan could be defined as use of the political process to acquire Jammu and Kashmir.

Warfare

Warfare is used as an ultimate instrument to achieve foreign policy goals. But in the case of Kashmir, Pakistan decided to use in the very beginning. Three attempts were made by Pakistan to win Kashmir through warfare.

Attempt in 1947

In 1947, vexed by the neutrality and dilemma of the Maharaja, Pakistan government forces launched massive attack on Jammu and Kashmir. The military attack was carried out under the pretext of freedom struggle, and their modus operandi was hit-n-run border incursions.

The tribes fighters from NWFP were organized at different places under the command of Pakistan's military personnel. On October 22, 1947, these fighters armed with modern weapons like Bren guns, Sten guns, grenades, heavy mortars, anti-tank rifles and an unlimited supply of ammunitions were brought to Muzzaffarabad in 300 lorries under the command of Major General Akbar Khan who was nicknamed General Tariq. The operation started with looting, plundering and arson leaving behind a trail of destruction wherever they passed through. The Pakistani-backed raiders fought their way to Baramullah, a town in the vicinity of Srinagar. [30] The level of plunder and arson was so horrifying that local the Muslim population along with the Indian military raised a war cry against Pakistan. They openly declared Pakistan as the aggressor and applauded Sheikh Abdullah for the accession decision of the state to India. Some of the most widely used slogans during this period were: *Hamlawar Hoshiyar, Hum Kashmiri Hain Taiyar* (Aggressor, beware. We Kashmiris are prepared) and *Sher-e-Kashmir Ki Kya Irshad, Hindu Muslim Sikh Ittehad* (The call of the Sheer-e-Kashmir is unity amongst Hindu, Muslim, and Sikh). [31]

The forces of Maharaja, however, were too weak to repel the armed aggression. The Maharaja thus had no option but to seek support from India. It was at this stage that Indian troops were flown to Srinagar to rescue the Kashmir from further pillage. The armed forces of both counties were now entangled in a long war of attrition in Jammu and Kashmir until the UN intervened in January 1948. A cease-fire was declared and, temporarily, the war came to an end. However, Pakistan had already captured 83,294 square kilometers of territory of the state. Instead of pushing Pakistani troops back to the pre-war position, an arbitrary Cease Fire Line (CFL) was declared which left approximately half of the state territory under the occupation of Pakistan.

Thus, Pakistan was successful in its mission to seize a portion of Kashmir through warfare. Almost half of the state territory went to Pakistan as is tabulated in Table 5. [32]

Table 5. Territory of Jammu and Kashmir

Total Area	222,236 sq km
Under Pak Occupation	78,114 sq km
Given to China by Pakistan	5,180 sq km
Occupied by China	37,555 sq km

Despite, the fact that the Pak-occupied territory is part of the Indian Union, it comes under jurisdiction of the Pakistan government for all practical purpose and CFL is accepted as the boundary line between India and Pakistan and is declared the Line of Control (LoC).

Attempt in 1965

The period between 1948 and 1965 witnessed major strategic alignment of forces among the world powers. The strategic move that brought landmark changes in India's foreign policy agenda was the 1962 Chinese attack. It was the beginning of strategic change in the political equation among nation-states in South Asia. Loss of Indian territory to China in the 1962 war and the sudden alignment in Sino-Pak relations was a let down India. Pakistan, after having judged the weaknesses of the Indian military in 1962, once again took cudgel against India's claim on Jammu and Kashmir.

With the help of defense supplies from the West and, after having taken China into confidence, Pakistan was set for a war with India. On the other hand, the Indian army, having suffered a massive set back in the 1962 war was unaware of the war preparations taking place across the Indo-Pak border. Armed with US$ 2.5 billion worth of tanks, jet fighters and other weapons from the U.S., Pakistan launched an attack on India in April 1965 in the Runn of Kutch. [33] This war ended with the signing of the Agreement for Arbitration in the Runn of Kutch on June 30, 1965. This agreement gave India a false impression, and Indian forces relapsed into peacetime postures. [34] While Pakistani forces were no merely reorganized, but a new force named Al Mujahid was created in addition to the existing strength.

The creation of Al Mujahid forces was exclusively designed to conquer Kashmir. It comprised of Kashmiri recruits form PoK. A division of this force called Al Burq was created to carry subversive activities in the valley. The recruits were trained in PoK by Chinese instructors in the art of sabotage and espionage[35] clearly defining Pakistan's objective in Jammu and Kashmir.

Thus Pakistan's invasion of Kashmir in 1965 was aimed at two directions—subversion and conventional war. General Kaul elaborates it in the following lines:

> About 10,000 infiltrators who were fully armed Pakistani soldiers in civilian dress under the command of Major General Akhtar Hussain Mulllick, GOC 12 divisions, slipped across the 470 mile long Cease Fire Line on August 5th through many gaps and trails. The infiltrators had eight commands with names like Gibraltar, Gaznavi and Salaluddin, each of the eight companies of 110 men trained in guerrilla warfare were commanded by regular army officers. They were equipped with light automatic weapons, and excellent wireless communication. Their aim, apart from sabotage was to indoctrinate the Kashmiris to revolt against India. [36]

However, this initiative of Pakistan did not succeed. Kashmiris did not sway by the call to rebellion and the objective of Pakistan to achieve Kashmir by subversion was defeated in 1965. The reason for this defeat, according to Pakistani General Musa, was inappropriate time and inadequate preparation. He believed that their plan of action was not even appraised to the pro-Pakistan elements in the valley. He held General Akhtar Hussain Mullick, commander of Azad Kashmir troops, responsible for this untimely action. He believed that General Mullick pressured the government to exploit the turbulent situation created by the arrest of Sheikh Abdullah and Mirza Afzal Beg in the valley.[37]

When they failed to create conditions favorable to their interst in the Kashmir valley, they turned towards the Chamb Jaurean sector in Akhnoor and Jammu region. The operation was code named Operation Grand Slam and the attack was launched on September 1, 1965. Pakistan forces reached Jaurean to capture Akhnoor along the river Chamb. Their plan was to cut the line of communication from Jammu to Poonch and occupy the Jammu-Srinagar highway. [38] This attempt too was defeated and Pakistani forces could not advance beyond the CFL. Thus, their bid to capture Jammu and Kashmir had failed once again.

Attempt in 1971

The third attempt to conquer Jammu and Kashmir by warfare was in 1971, when the forces of both countries were engaged in war for the liberation of Bangladesh, the former East Pakistan. Pakistan had no chance of winning this war because India had joined hands with the Mukti Bahini. General Yahya Khan, the former President and military dictator of Pakistan was fully aware that they were fighting a lost battle. In order to compensate this loss, he decided to capture a sizable portion of Jammu and Kashmir in the western front.[39]

As a preparatory measure, Pakistan frequently violated CFL by deliberately sending spies and agents from Pak-occupied Kashmir. They seized the territory by deceit, occupied vacant land, send in villagers, who hurriedly built thatched huts, tilled and cultivated the land and ultimately claimed it as their territory.[40]

This was followed by attacks on the airfield and radar installation at Srinagar on 3rd December 1971. Then PoK battalions infiltrated into Indian territory and fought with Indian forces. This move was also aimed at capturing Indian bases in Kashmir. The plan was to isolate towns and cut important routes through which Indian troops could counter-attack.[41]

But all these attempts were frustrated by the India forces as information from various sources had alerted them well in advance. The Indian army camps in Jammu and Kashmir were flooded with intelligence information that there was large-scale movement of Pakistani troops in Muzzaffarabad and other bordering areas.[42]

Meanwhile, Pakistan lost the war in Bangladesh, and on December 16, 1971, General Niazi signed the Instrument of Surrender. The humiliating defeat of Pakistani forces in the Bangladesh war led to the end of war in Jammu and Kashmir as well. And thus, once again, Pakistan had failed to acquire the state through warfare.

Limited War in Kargil, 1999

After the Bangladesh war, India and Pakistan signed the Shimla Agreement in 1972. It was agreed that both countries would respect LoC. But with the help of Afghan Mujahideens, the Pakistan army often ventured across the LoC to capture Jammu and Kashmir. However, no serious incursion took place until January 1999. While India was looking for a peaceful relationship with Pakistan after the 1998 nuclear test, the Pakistan army planned to capture

Kargil and Drass sectors of Kashmir. It is critical to note that during winter, the Indian army abandons some posts on top of the mountains because of weather conditions. This arrangement was exploited by the Mujahideens and the Pakistan army in the late 1990s. In a well-planned move, they captured this region. In response, the Indian air force struck Pakistani bunkers in Kargil and Drass sectors of Kashmir resulting in limited war between India and Pakistan. Though Pakistan did not declare war against India because of international pressure, a limited war was fought with Pakistan to recapture the entire region. Indian soldiers proved their bravery and skill when they captured the Tiger Hill, the most vital point for Pakistan, on July 4, 1999, and finally pushed the defeated Pakistan troops back into their country.

The Pakistan government realized the miscalculation of ISI and military. Nawaz Sharief rushed to Washington for help and finally agreed to retreat his forces but only when they had been pushed back by the Indian forces and after heavy casualties on both sides.

As a matter of fact, the 1999 adventure by Pakistan would go down in the history of the Indian sub-continent, as the first time that Pakistan was isolated and condemned by the international community including China, a traditional ally of Pakistan. Thus, once again Pakistan failed to achieve its objective in Jammu and Kashmir in limited war with India in 1999.

In October 2001, Pakistan troops again provoked India by mounting cross-border attacks on Kashmir. However, it is obvious that as in the past, Pakistan will not succeed in its objective to grab Kashmir from India. The irony is that while on one hand, Pakistan is supposedly an ally with the U.S. in fighting terrorism in Afghanistan; on the other hand, Pakistan continues to support terrorist attacks on India.

The United Nations
The UN is the prominent international organization that looks into international disputes. It is the only existing body that could be used by member nations to settle disputes at the international forum.

So, India was right to raise the Kashmir issue before the UN. However, Pakistan has utilized the international organization to gain favor from the international community. Pakistan's Foreign Ministry Zafarullah Khan presented his case so brilliantly that delegates to the UN in 1948 interpreted the problem of Kashmir as an international extension of the communal conflict that had given birth to Pakistan. [43]

Only time will tell if Pakistan has been successful in its efforts at the UN. But the truth is that Pakistan has used the international organization to try to grab Jammu and Kashmir.

The Kashmir problem was brought to the UN on January 1, 1948 by India with the hope that international community would pronounce Pakistan the aggressor. In response to India's presentation, Pakistan requested the Security Council for a stay of proceedings to prepare for the case [44] because the Pakistani leaders were not even prepared to discuss an international debate on the Kashmir issue.

As it turned out, India's well-intentioned representation to the UN provided another opportunity for Pakistan to claim Jammu and Kashmir through international mediation. India's expectations that the UN would condemn Pakistan for its aggression in Jammu and Kashmir turned sour when world opinion was divided on the subject. After a series of debates and discussion from both parties, the UN Commission for India and Pakistan (UNCIP) was formed. [45]

Both countries, at this stage, were engaged in war at two different fronts—one at the battlefield and the other at the UN. While the war continued to challenge the security of Jammu and Kashmir, the representations, were busy debating it in the UN.

India demanded a cessation of war, whereas Pakistan insisted on a plebiscite. The general opinion, after hearing the two representations, was so divided that the Security Council drafted two resolutions simultaneously. [46]

The idea of two resolutions was welcomed by Pakistan, but was severely criticized by the Indian representative, Gopalkrishna Ayyangar, who described the whole exercise as "fiddling while Kashmir is burning." [47] Arguments and counter-arguments from both the sides continued until the Security Council passed the UNCIP resolution on January 13, 1948, which called for a cease-fire and the demilitarization of the entire state to conduct free and impartial plebiscite in order to ascertain the wishes of the people.

It is important to mention here that by the time this resolution was enforced, Pakistan had already usurped almost half of the territory of the state. The UN resolution for immediate cease-fire and subsequent demarcation of CFL divided the state into two.

Pakistan agreed to the proposal because is held power and authority over the occupied territory (PoK) and named it Azad Kashmir. Though the Security Council resolution advocated demilitarization, it was inconceivable that Pakistan would ever withdraw from the PoK. As a matter of fact, the implementation of this resolution further debilitated the case of India, and for all practical purposes Pakistan's administration prevailed upon in PoK. India, thus, lost half of the state to Pakistan at the UN which could have could have been saved by military action. The spirit of the Indian army at that time was high enough to recapture Kashmir. The spirit was so high that Baramullah, which had been captured by Pakistan, was recaptured by the Indian Army. [48] Leaders were also positive in their approach to a military solution. Had that spirit been converted into military action Azad Kashmir would not have come into being. But once the UN mediation began and up to date, the matter remains unresolved.

General McNaughton of Canada, the former president of the Security Council, was the first UN sponsored mediator appointed to settle the Kashmir problem. He suggested demilitarization and UN supervision for conducting a plebiscite. The idea of demilitarization was rejected by Pakistan, while India refused to abide by the proposal for UN administration of the state until a plebiscite was conducted.

This was followed by the proposal by Owen Dixon, the UN representative for India and Pakistan. He recommended a solution that did not include conducting plebiscite. [49] He proposed a plan which suggested division of the state on certain principles: (1) no plebiscite on those areas where it was obvious that people would accede to either of the two domination, (2) a plebiscite should be limited to those areas where there is no certainty, and (3) demarcation of the state should have regard for geographical features as is required for an international boundary. In the third point, India was willing, but Pakistan refused because it wanted the valley to be handed over in totality, which India rejected.

Dixon was succeeded by Franc Graham in 1953 who also laid emphasis on demilitarization of the state. But this too could not break the ice.

All the UN sponsored measures failed to bring the two contenders to an agreement. Hence these efforts went in vain and part of Kashmir remained occupied by Pakistan. These efforts by

Pakistan could be defined as use of an international organization to try to acquire Jammu and Kashmir.

Diplomacy and Propaganda

The first diplomatic maneuver of Pakistan towards the acquisition of Kashmir started soon after the accession of Jammu and Kashmir to India. Jinnah invited Mountabatten and Nehru to a Conference in Lahore. While Nehru did not attend, Mountbatten, in his capacity as the first Governor General of independent India, proceeded to Lahore. His first proposal to Jinnah was for simultaneous withdrawal of troops from the state; and second was for a plebiscite under UN supervision. Jinnah refused to comply with either of the two. The outcome of the conference was an impass.[50] Determined to acquire Jammu and Kashmir, Jinnah ordered his armed forces to invade the state but he was compelled to withdraw the order when Field Marshall Sir Claude Auchenleck, the Supreme Commander of all British forces in South Asia, explained to the Pakistani premier that since accession of Kashmir to India was legal, any Pakistani order to invade a sister Commonwealth country would lead to the withdrawal of British troops serving in Pakistan.[51] Thus the war continued in the guise of tribal invasion until the Cease Fire was announced.

Bilateral Diplomacy

The UN representatives made in clear that bilateral negotiations was the only way to solve the Kashmir problem. The first direct negotiations took place on June 5, 1953 in London. This was not of much significance except for the fact that both parties agreed to resume talks. The second talks started in Karachi on July 25, 1953, in an amicable environment where both parties expressed satisfaction because they agreed to the demilitarization and to conducting a plebiscite. The third negotiation took place on August 17, 1953, in New Delhi. The contenders resolved to set up a Plebiscite Administrator. But these efforts failed because of the configuration of world forces and Pakistan's joining hands with Western-sponsored military organizations like SEATO and CENTO. Nehru considered Pakistan's decision to join the U.S.-sponsored military alliances as a negative, dangerous and harmful approach.[52] And hence he declined to conduct the plebiscite.

In the process of direct negotiations, time passed and no

breakthrough was achieved, as it is obvious from the report submitted on April 29, 1957, by Semeour Jennings, President of the Security Council.

After a period of 10 years—1948-1958—and the military alliance joined by Pakistan provided enough justification for Nehru to declare accession of Kashmir as irrevocable and final.

This statement by Nehru received sever criticism. But considering the amount of efforts he put into conducting a plebiscite from 1948 to 1955, it would but be unfair to condemn a shift in his approach towards Pakistan after 1954. It must not be forgotten that until 1954, it was Nehru who forcefully advocated the idea of conducting a plebiscite, while his counterpart in Pakistan kept refusing. The constant refusal by Pakistan is well manifested in the speech by Feroz Khan Noon in the Pakistan Constituent Assembly when he stated that: "If our government is looking towards the UN for a plebiscite, I regret to say that they are looking in vain." [53] But in his capacity as the Foreign Minister of Pakistan, Noon later approached the Security Council in 1957 to discuss a plebiscite. It was a clear example of a diplomatic summersault as far as Pakistan's policy towards for problem of Kashmir is concerned.

Beside the military alliance and the recalcitrant approach of Pakistani leaders, a period of 6 years—1948 to 1954—is considerably a long period to affect the economy of a nation constantly plagued with wars of retribution. Special economic measures were adopted by the government of India to safeguard security and integrity of Kashmir. Leave alone the constant use of terrorism, overt war itself incurred heavy financial liability. Under these circumstances, and considering that the people of Kashmir had already exercised their democratic rights the in 1951 general elections, the shift in India's commitment to conduct a plebiscite was justified. But, it left behind far reaching impact on Indo-Pak relations.

The causes for failure of bilateral diplomacy to resolve the Indo-Pak conflict over Kashmir could be attributed to the following factors: (1) inherent contradictions in the dispute over Kashmir, (2) Pakistan's alliance with the military forces which, according the Nehru, was denial of demilitarization as agreed upon by both countries and (3) Pakistan's refusal to sign the "No War Pact" which was proposed by India thrice—1949-50, 1953-54 and 1956.[54]

The outcome of the failure of bilateral negotiations was continued occupation of PoK by Pakistan. There was no change whatsoever in Pakistan's territorial status over the Jammu and Kashmir. Practically, Pakistan affirmed its authority over occupied territory.

The only landmark achievement in the bilateral negotiation was the Shimla Agreement. Pakistan agreed to sign the accord because of immediate post-war problems. This agreement had several weaknesses. Before discussing the weaknesses of the Shimla Agreement, it is helpful to highlight salient features of the agreement which are as follows:

The principles and purpose of the UN Charter shall govern.
Respect for territorial integrity, sovereignty and non interference.
Prevention of hostile propaganda.
Resumption of communication and tavel facilities.
LoC to be respected by both the parties.
Repatriation of Prisoners of War (POW).[55]

The weaknesses of the Shimla Agreement could be traced back to the fact that the agreement was not signed in a harmonious environment. The Pakistan government was panic-stricken and preoccupied with the crisis of its POWs. Some 90,000 Pakistani soldiers had surrendered to the Joint Indo-Bangla forces after the defeat in the 1971 war. Bhutto was under tremendous pressure to get the POWs released as expediently as possible.

Under such circumstances the Pakistan government had no option but to sign the agreement. Except for the repatriation of the POWs, none of the principles, as laid down in the agreement were respected by the Pakistani leaders. While on one hand preparation for Shimla Agreement was progressing, Pakistani forces on the other hand, attacked Titwal Sector of jammu and Kashmir on May 5, 1972, and violated the CFL in Rajouri and Poonch Sectors.[56] As if that were not enough, before leaving for Shimla, Bhutto, when speaking at Hussaini Wala and other forward areas on June 27, 1972, made it clear that the Kashmir issue would be raised again once the POWs were repatriated.

On the other hand, India adopted a positive approach after the victory in the 1971 war. India's foreign policy objective (creation of Bangladesh) was achieved, and policy makers were in a buoyant mood. But international opinion was running high against India's involvement in the creation of Bangladesh and hence Indian leaders were keen to compromise of the issue of Line of Control (LoC) in Kashmir.

Territorial integrity was on top of the Indian agenda, because in the Kargil division, a 250-miles long highway linking Srinagar with Leh, run parallel to the Cease Fire Line, which is vulnerable to attacks from Pakistani pickets, lodged in the high mountains.[57] The priority to maintain territorial integrity was also emphasized by international envoys like Galbraith who clearly stated that Pakistan should not raise the question of a plebiscite as there was no future in this hypothesis.[58]

The weaknesses of the agreement could be also seen in the light of the fact that along with territorial integrity, LoC was also agreed upon as the boundary line between the two for all practical purposes.

The Shimla Agreement, thus, did not let Pakistan's position down on the subject of Jammu and Kashmir. On the contrary, it successfully persuaded India to accept CFL as LoC. In other words, Pakistan compelled India to surrender PoK. This agreement gave legal sanction to Pakistan's claim on PoK.

At this stage of the development in Jammu and Kashmir, Pakistan was poised for utilization of various diplomatic channels to acquire the state. These efforts, nevertheless, were more in the form of propaganda at multilateral level of diplomacy rather than real diplomatic endeavor. This aspect is discussed in the following section.

Propaganda at Multilateral Diplomacy
After having acquired legal sanction of PoK—half of the total area of Jammu and Kashmir, Pakistani leaders switched over to propaganda at the international level to acquire the entire state of Jammu and Kashmir.

The failure in bilateral negotiations, as mentioned earlier, gave an impression to politicians in Pakistan that India's position on Kashmir was firm and that the state could not be acquired unless there was overwhelming support from the world community. One of the effective tools to create this awareness was to hop on claims of violation of human rights and on the need to conduct a plebiscite in the state. The same was employed to woo public opinion during the first phase of negotiations on Kashmir. It needs to be remembered that Liaquat Ali Khan had virtually canceled his trip to London to attend the Commonwealth Conference to be held in January 1951, on the grounds that Kashmir did not appear in the agenda of the Conference. It was only after assurance for an informal discussion on Kashmir from the British Prime Minister, Attlee, that he attended the conference. [59] It was only after assurance for an informal discussion on Kashmir from the British Prime Minister did not take place in a hotel and outside the official agenda of the Commonwealth Conference. This meeting also proposed direct negotiation between the two parties. Nothing came out of Liaquat Ali's efforts.

Later, after having joined military blocks and having had the experience of a deadlock in the bilateral negotiations, Pakistan decided to advocate for the cause of Kashmir at different international organizations. Diplomatic privileges were used for propaganda. Hamidul Haq, the Foreign Minister of Pakistan, raised the Kashmir issue while attending a SEATO meeting and asked them to support Pakistan's demand for a plebiscite. [60] It needs to be emphasized here that though propaganda was used extensively by the Pakistani leaders specifically to influence Muslim nations the Asian nations remained neutral on Kashmir. For instance, the former Prime Minister of Indonesia, Mohammad Hutta stated, "Indonesia is an Asian rather than an Islamic state." Similarly, the general opinion in Turkey, a member of CENTO, was, "Turkey is governed by civil rather than religious law." [61] Likewise, the government of Malyasia maintained that the Kashmir dispute needed to be solved through bilateral negotiation. The Malaysian leaders dismissed Pakistan's position that the Kashmir issue was related to problem of Islam.

In the Gulf countries, Pakistan also gradually lost favor in the wake of the Suez Crisis in 1956. Bhutto tried to regain the lost image at the Summit Meetings of Muslim Heads of State held at Rabat, Morocco in 1969 and at Jedah and Karachi in 1970. He strongly supported the idea of forming the Organization of Islamic Conference (OIC) which came into being in May 1971. The creation of OIC served two purposes in Pakistan's foreign policy agenda. First, it helped Pakistan regain the support of Arab countries, which Pakistan had lost in the midst of the Suez Crisis.

Second, this forum was used by Pakistan to exploit sentiments of Muslims for the cause of Kashmir. Ever since the creation of OIC, Pakistan has used this forum for propaganda on Kashmir, but has never achieved success because India maintains friendly relations with many Arab and Islamic countries. [62]

Foreign Assistance

Pakistan is an agrarian country with low per capita income, (though little higher than India) and the country is yet to explore its full potential for economic growth. Under such a poor state of economic affairs, Pakistan cannot afford to challenge India's territorial integrity unless it receives assistance from abroad. Foreign assistance comes in two ways—in financial and economic aid and in support for strengthening its defense capability. Thus foreign assistance could be classified in two categories: (a) economic assistance and (b) military assistance.

Both these facilities have been used by Pakistan to achieve its foreign policy goal in Jammu and Kashmir. The external aid given to Pakistan by Arabs and Americans for economic development is siphoned to Kashmiri militants. Pakistani leaders have been so enthusiastic to create unrest in the valley of Kashmir that a special Kashmir cell was set up. Money and defense equipment were supplied to militants through party offices. [63]

However, since these funds came indirectly, it is difficult to back up the claim with documentary evidence. But when comparing the amount of funds sanctioned to Pakistan from external agencies, to the insignificant economic growth and heavy expenditure on arms and ammunition for militancy in Kashmir, it becomes clear that funds for development aid are used by Pakistan to pursue its goals in Jammu and Kashmir.

Of the two types of foreign aid, military assistance played an important role in the low intensity conflict. The supply of defense equipment as well as mercenary training provided to Kashmiri militants by the Pakistan army are an integral part of military assistance provided to terrorists active in Jammu and Kashmir.

During the period of Soviet expansionism, the U.S. was looking for a base in the Indian sub-continent to challenge the Soviet plans for South Asia. Pakistan was willing to accept this proposition provided the flow of economic and military aid was ensured. India, on the other hand, championed the cause of nonalignment and was in no way looking towards the U.S. for military aid. Pakistan, thus, found itself in an opportune position to fit into U.S. objectives in the region and become a frontline state against expansion of Soviet Communism. It was the only way through which Pakistan could acquire sophisticated weapons and defense equipment to strengthen its defense forces against India.

Much has been written and debated on the issue of U.S. interests in supplying weapons and defense equipment to Pakistan and the latter's objective to receive it. But it does not need to be reiterated that Pakistan received weapons to fight against India. The supply of these weapons inspired Pakistan to try to settle the Kashmir dispute by force as it is obvious from the 1965 adventure of Pakistan in Jammu and Kashmir.

Further political developments in this region, particularly the Soviet invasion of Afghanistan in 1979, intensified Pakistan's hankering for sophisticated weapons. Pakistan found the event to be a good opportunity to bargain with the U.S. Alarmed by the Soviet expansionist designs, the U.S. flooded Pakistan with a variety of high-tech defense equipment at the rate of five hundred million dollars per year. The annual flow of sophisticated arms into Pakistan during this period (1979-1982) is estimated at one billion dollars.[64]

The international scenario, however, was not favorable enough for a declared war against India. But Bhutto and his successor, General Zia-ul-Huq did use these weapons for abetting terrorism in Jammu and Kashmir. It is because of foreign assistance that General Zia-ul-Huq organized bases for military training for subversion in the valley. This aspect will be highlighted in the following section which elaborates use of terrorism by Pakistan to capture Kashmir.

TERRORISM: AN ULTIMATE INSTRUMENT

After having tried all the above-mentioned conventionally acceptable means to achieve foreign policy goals, Pakistan did succeed in a partial takeover of the state hence Azad Kashmir. But its overall goal, to acquire the entire state, has not been achieved to date.

The change of the equation in Indo-Pak relations from 1954 onwards—the signing of Shimla Agreement in 1972, the disintegration of the Soviet Union in 1991, end of the Cold War, and defeat of Pakistan in the limited war at Kargil in 1999—do not indicate that Pakistan would ever achieve Kashmir, through conventional instruments of foreign policy.

The two nations appeared to have resolved the conflict through the Shimla Agreement. However, the issues agreed upon remained only on paper. The clauses that adversely affected Pakistan's objective in Kashmir were soon renounced without any reservation to the commitments made at Shimla. Also, except for the resumption of communication facilities and repatriation of POWs, none of the clauses in the Shimla Agreement were implemented by the Pakistan government.

Pakistan maintained a low profile for couple of years after the Shimla Agreement. It did not intervene in Jammu and Kashmir aggressively. But as soon as the POWs were repatriated by April 1974, Pakistan's attitude towards India changed.

Meanwhile, Indian politics entered into a phase of instability which directly affected the Kashmir problem. The large scale rigging of the 1987 Assembly Election of Jammu and Kashmir was the flash point that put the central government in the dock. The people of Kashmir were disgusted and the government of India was losing credibility. There was an outburst of mass anxiety. People now started thinking that the central government didn't care for people's rights in Kashmir and installs puppet governments which don't represent the masses. The popular sentiments mounted high against India, which was precipitated by negligence of the central government. Jagmohan rightly points out that "it is not Kalasnikov that kills, it is also the indifference casualness and negligence that destroy without being visible."[65]

The turbulent situation in the valley gave Pakistan an opportunity to exploit the political turmoil in pursuit of the realization of its foreign policy goals. In total violation of the Shimla Agreement, Pakistan indulged in massive propaganda through mass media; and encouraged disgruntled youth of the valley to join terrorist activities. The unemployed youth population of the valley was lured into the hazardous profession. They were trained in subversion and made self-styled commanders or generals of different militant outfits. The Pakistan authorities, however, did not receive enthusiastic support from the masses until the 1980s.

It was only when the government of India appeared to have lost its credentials that the Pakistan government geared its machinery to alienate the Muslim population of Jammu and Kashmir from India. The ongoing political movement was henceforth given a communal window dressing. The political grievances of people were covered in an Islamic cloak. Islamic religious propaganda was disseminated which had a far-reaching impact on the young population of the valley. The young school dropouts and unemployed graduates were turned on to the violent course of action. They were no merely converted to fight for Islam and become martyrs, but also given opportunities to work as professional with wages. Both these factors became alchemists for terrorism in Kashmir. Pakistan was now poised to sponsor these young people in the valley to conquer Jammu and Kashmir though terrorism. The following section analyzes Pakistan's design to alienate the state from India.

The Operation Tupac
Cross-border terrorism is not an easy task to be carried out through normal government machinery. As a member of the UN, Pakistan is answerable for any indulgence in unconventional warfare if proven guilty. General Zia was conscious of this international obligation. Hence he set an agenda and formulated a long-term plan that could serve the objective of Pakistan in Jammu and Kashmir without damaging its credentials in the international forum.

Inspired by Tupac Amin, an Inca Prince who fought non-conventional war against Spanish Rule in 18th century Uruguay, General Zia implemented an idea which is identified by the Indian defense analysts as Operation Tupac. [66] This is a controversial code name as there is no official proof to substantiate its existence. But the history of Tupac Amin and what happened in Kashmir, if analyzed thoroughly, leads to the conclusion that Zia-ul-Huq did use Tupac Amin's approach in a very systematic way in the fight for Kashmir against the government of India. The aim of this operation was to wrestle Jammu and Kashmir from India. Zia believed that what Pakistan could not achieve through wars in 1948, 1965 and 1971 could be achieved through subversion, force and religious fanaticism. [67]

The action, plan, as proposed was to be implemented in three phases: The first phase was directed towards insurgency against the local regimes to disrupt the government machinery. The idea was to place the stage on siege from within without inviting imposition of central rule. This mission was partly successful in the sense that the state government collapsed. However, the enforcement of central rule could not be avoided and this went against the Pakistani design.

The second phase was to exert pressure on the Siachin, Kargil and Rajouri-Poonch sectors so that concentration of the Indian army would be out side the main valley. But Pakistan could not get the breakthrough in this strategy because the Indian army maintained strong holds in the state except for some intelligence lapses in the Kargil and Drass sectors.

The third phase was preparation for the liberation of Kashmir valley from India. In order to gain overwhelming support from the Kashmiri people, it was also proposed that after the liberation, steps would be taken for establishment of an independent Islamic state. The word "independent" was added purposely to ensure active participation of the local people.

The implementation of this plan was entrusted to different intelligence agencies in Pakistan which provide infrastructure facilities for terrorism in Jammu and Kashmir. Before analyzing sources of infrastructure, it is appropriate to present a list of terrorism related incidents of crime in the state, which clearly shows that, to a great extent, Pakistan successfully implemented Operation Tupac.

The figures from 1981 to 1989 clearly show a continuous increase in number of crimes. However, because of the unavailability of information, it is difficult to confirm whether these incidents of crime were directly related to terrorism in the valley or are crimes of ordinary nature. Bit it is apparent that most of the incidents of crime that took place during 1980-1990 were terrorism-related crimes. This was the period when Pakistan was actively abetting terrorism in the state. Table 6 presents number of incidents of crime in the state during this period.[68]

Table 6: Incidents of cognizable crimes (IPC) under different crime heads in Jammu and Kashmir, 1980-1990*

Year	Total Incidents Of Crime	Murder	Attempt To Murder	Kid-napping	Dacoity	Under TADA
1980	-	100	7	473	13	-
1981	15,973	90	7	475	10	-
1982	15,523	91	10	449	10	-
1983	17,139	103	8	461	33	-

1984	17,022	120	9	458	25	-
1985	19,440	121	9	544	6	-
1986	19,055	87	9	509	-	-
1987	19,158	102	12	517	18	-
1988	19,868	111	368	525	17	36
1989	21,442	119	505	532	17	163
1990	15,047	546	454	347	21	1498

Source: *Crime in India*, National Crime Record Bureau, Vol. 1980 to 1990, (New Delhi).

The table shows that the total number of incidents of crime increased except in 1990. The decrease in the total number of crimes in 1990 is because of the approximately ten times increase in crime under TADA, which was enforced in 1987. Other incidents of crime decreased because the concentration was more towards terrorist activities than crime of general nature.

These figures are manifestation of reign of terror unleashed by Pakistan in the Kashmir Valley. It is, thus, significant to highlight infrastructure facilities provided to militants in Kashmir, which mainly come through Pakistan's intelligence agencies.[69]

Model V highlights sources of infrastructure for terrorism in Jammu and Kashmir.

Model V
Sources of Infrastructure for Terrorism in Jammu and Kashmir

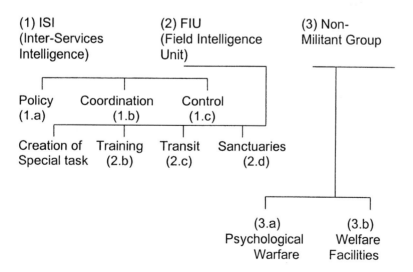

Inter Service Intelligence (ISI)

Pakistan's ISI is empowered to deal with both internal and external matters. It has a double role to play that makes ISI an important agency in establishing links between the government of Pakistan and the Kashmiri terrorists. The ISI is given discretionary power to deal with affairs related to terrorism in India. Political coordination and control are two major issues that come within the discretionary power of ISI.

The task of ISI is to formulate policy in consultation with militant outfits. Numerically, it is not yet clear how many terrorist groups are active in the valley. Sources confirm that approximately 20 groups are operating in the state. Some of these could be identified as:

1. JKLF	9. The Muslim Janbaz Force
2. Jamat-I-Islami	10. Ikhwane Muslimeen
3. Hizbul Mujahideen	11. Allah Tigers
4. Students Liberation Front	12. Hizb-ul-Islami
5. Mahaz-e-Azadi	13. Harket-al-Jehad / Ansar
6. Islamic Students League	14. Lakshar-I-Toiba
7. People's League	15. Markaz-I-Dawaul Irshad
8. Islamic Jamat-e-Tulba	(MDI) (active in Kargil)

The first eight groups were banned in the valley on April 16, 1990, under the state's Criminal Law Enactment Act. The rest are operating from Pakistan. They all receive policy direction form the ISI.

The second important task of ISI is coordination, which is a must in subversion. Coordination is important to maintain linkage between the actors and perpetrators. The ISI keeps constant vigil on activities of militants and the civilian government, and accordingly maintains coordination.

It also coordinates between the suppliers of weapons and terrorist groups. The kind of weapons to be sold, mode of payment and delivery of the goods are negotiated directly under the aegis of the ISI. It is relevant to note in this context that rockets, light and heavy guns, have a controlled supply and are meant for specialized groups only.[70]

Last, but not least significant, is the coordination amongst various terrorist groups active in the valley. There are innumerable splinter groups that operate simultaneously. Their activities are under the vigilance of intelligence agencies of India. Terrorists could become victims of their own design in the hands of Indian armed forces. This risk is well taken care of by the ISI in coordination with Field Intelligence Unit (FIU). They safeguard interests of terrorist groups by maintaining coordination and warning them in advance about movements of the Indian intelligence and Bangladeshi Security personnel.

The third important task assigned to the ISI is that of control. While providing logistic support, the sponsoring country cannot afford to endanger its own security. Thus overall control of terrorist activities becomes essential. Militants, if left undeterred, can pose threats to the Pakistan government itself; and thus their activities are monitored by the ISI.

However, the role of the ISI in abetting terrorism is more prominent in Punjab and other states of India than in Jammu and Kashmir. It is the Field Intelligence Unit (FIU) which carries subversion in Jammu and Kashmir. Its contribution is analyzed in the following section.

Field Intelligence Unit (FIU)

The FIU is the most important Pakistan intelligence unit which provides infrastructure facilities for terrorism in Jammu and Kashmir. From its bases in PoK, the FIU provides logistic support and training to terrorists who create unrest in Kashmir.

The FIU's first and foremost assigned duty is to form special action groups to carry out acts of terrorism in Jammu and Kashmir. The recruitment of members for this special task force is done by FIU. Because it is on field duty, FIU keeps direct contact with the incoming refugees. This direct contact keeps FIU members abreast of an individual's potentiality and level of crusading zeal. ISI does not have direct contact with people crossing the border. It functions from behind the scenes. Thus, FIU is empowered to take independent decisions on matters of recruitment. The Pakistani agents belonging to FIU are on record as having abducted 85 villagers from Karni village (Indian side) on August 28, 1991 in Poonch, and inducted them in terrorist groups. This zone is vulnerable for forced recruitment as LoC runs in a direction where 60 percent of the homes lie within the Pakistan boundary, 30 percent in India and 10 percent in the disputed territory. [71] This situation is favorable for FIU. They force youth of the villages to join terrorist groups by threatening the peace of their family and, by giving financial support. Abdul Hamid Gani, a twenty-year-old teacher from Kupwara district revealed that he was picked up when his brother did not pay a ransom of Rs. 20,000. [72] By using such coercive methods the FIU created a Special Task Force.

After the creation of the Task Force, the next phase is to train the recruits. Most of the militants crossing from the Kashmir valley to the Pakistan side do not have the necessary background for militancy and are just innocent school boys. [73] Some of them actually get the opportunity to see weapons for the first time in their lives. Training, thus, becomes an important aspect for sponsored terrorism. These facilities are provided by FIU in different camps set up in PoK under command of regular Pakistan army officers. It needs to be emphasized that only training facilities, not training per se is provided by the FIU.

The most crucial task, however, allotted to FIU is to provide information for safe transit of terrorists and weapons into India. Special border contact groups and internal contact groups have been created for this purpose. These contact groups are operating both within and beyond the territory of Pakistan [74] and in coordination with Pakistani border rangers. Thus, the FIU plays the most active role in export of weapons and terrorists across the border in Jammu and Kashmir.

Besides these regular operations of the FIU to provide support bases and transit, Pakistan armed forces also give cover up military operations for safe infiltrations or terrorists in the valley. For instance, they frequently attacked Indian outposts and civilian locations in the state during August and September 1991. This was part of their tactics to divert the attention of Indian forces in the Kargil sector from the tightly guarded mountain routes in Uri and Kupwara sectors. These routes are used by Kashmiri terrorists. Pakistan armed forces often exchange fire with their Indian counterparts so that the terrorists can sneak through the Kargil sector. [75] In order to carry out all such activities, FIU plays a significant role, as it is always on field duty. The developments in June 1999 in the Kargil and Drass sectors also reveals the Pakistan continue to support infiltration into Indian territory.

Non-Militant Groups

Non-militant groups are other supporting agencies that provide infrastructure for terrorism in Jammu and Kashmir. These groups offer welfare services like supply or rations and medical facilities to terrorists. They also help in propagating religious fundamentalism. Some of the non-militant groups are semi-religious by nature, while some have political orientations.

The major concern of such groups is to create a psychological warfare, provide temporary sanctuary to militants after operations, indulge in propaganda and ensure welfare of their families. [76] These groups are more active in Jammu and Kashmir where Pakistan government plays the religion cards. Most of the heinous communal propaganda disseminated in the state are concocted by the non-militant groups.

The most important characteristic of these groups is common ideology. Because of co-religious identity, Kashmiri terrorists depend as much on non-militant sources for infrastructure as on the mercenary forces. The nature of the non-militant activities is very challenging in the sense that they create psychological warfare at the grass-roots level. People are swayed by the propaganda that helps terrorists to weaken the morale of local governments and alienate masses from the Indian mainstream.

TACTICS OF PAK-SPONSORED TERRORISM

After having discussed infrastructure facilities for Pak-sponsored terrorism in Jammu and Kashmir, it is also significant to examine tactics employed by Pakistani agents for export of terrorism in Kashmir.

The tactics of terrorism depends on the infrastructure facilities. All the tactics employed by Pakistan are in tune with the infrastructure, because tactics would not work if infrastructure is not available. Thus the tactics used by the Pakistan government to sponsor terrorism are the same as practiced by any terrorist groups in the world. These tactics could be described as follows.

The first tactic of Pakistan is alienation of Kashmir from the mainstream of India by dividing people into religious groups. [77] this is mainly done by propaganda at religious congregations and through mass media. Pakistan has been successful in the application of this tactic to a great extent. The communal division of people is clearly seen in the existing social conditions of the state. The Hindu population has migrated [78] from the valley and the

Muslims have lost faith in Kashmiri Pundits and Dogras. This tactic was vital for the success of Pakistan in Jammu and Kashmir as the masses are swayed by religious rhetoric.

The second tactic used by Pakistan is subversion of the state machinery, through violence, murder, arson, kidnapping, robbery and hijacking. All these tactics are employed by the Pakistan government to subvert the government. Bombs and hand grenades were extensively used by Kashmiri terrorists to destroy important offices and railways. Top ranking executives and officials were kidnapped and use to bargain for the release of terrorists arrested by the government of India. Robbery, drug trafficking and other tools of terror are used to accumulate funds for terrorist activities and to destroy the economy of the state. Hijackers are given protection on humanitarian grounds. All these tactics are used for subversion.

The third important terrorist tactic employed by Pakistan is related to infiltration of terrorists from PoK to Jammu and Kashmir.

The LoC has been accepted as the official line of control. Hence infiltration from PoK is illegal. The Indian army can shoot any one crossing LoC. This is a delicate issue in the sense that unless Pak-trained Kashmiri militants sneak into the Indian border in Kashmir, the foreign policy objective of Pakistan cannot be achieved. Thus, for safe intrusion of terrorists, the Pakistan army indulges in shootings and infringements with the Indian army to divert attention from the important passes between India and Pakistan. The geographical location, i.e. high mountains in the state, is such that terrorists cannot cross the border except from certain points, mainly in the Kupwara district, where Muslims constitute 97.53 percent of the population. An eye-witness account of a Kashmiri terrorist arrested by the Indian army while trying to go back to PoK in early 1993 reveals this fact. In his own words:

On September 13, 1991, we were prepared to move from Tejian (PoK) in the night. For three nights till September 18, the Pakistani army gave us covering fire. They were right behind us engaging the Indian security positions in a spate of counter-fire until we managed to sneak into Kupwara. [79]

Finally, an important tactic of Pakistan is to establish links with the Sikhs and Kashmiri terrorists. The ISI is trying to bring them together for joint action. The coordination between the two militant forces against India is important because Jammu and Kashmir has a sizable population of Sikhs that could be used by Pakistani leaders. The London based International Sikh Youth Federation (ISYF) is very active and have access to Gurudwaras abroad. Pakistan is trying to use them to revive terrorism in Punjab. [80] By forming an alliance between the two, Pakistan's tactic is to divert attention of the Indian army from both states so that government machinery collapses and civil war breaks out.

To conclude the foregoing discussion on sources of infrastructure and tactics for terrorism in Kashmir, it must be reiterated that Pakistan's vow to provide moral support to Kashmiri terrorists until their goal is realized needs special attention. The point of serious concern is, whose goal does Pakistan intend to achieve—JKLF's or its own? The cold response of the Sharief government to JKLF plan to cross the LoC during January to March 1992 and also in October 1999 is a vivid example of Pakistan's ambiguous approach towards human sufferings in Kashmir. It is important to add that state-sponsored terrorism is basically another name for a war of attrition between two rival governments. Public interest hardly comes into consideration. People are used as pawns in the hands of two players for power.

Finally, it is also relevant to note that the pro-Pakistan, Hizb-ul-Mujahideen, has threatened to punish JKLF for demanding Azadi 81 Hence Pakistan's defense for supporting terrorism in Kashmir does not have any logical justification. It is important, however, to also observe that justification itself is a controversial issue in Indo-Pak relations that are embodied in contradictions and dilemmas that exist in the politics of the two countries. Thus unless this thorn of contradiction is removed form the basic premise of their relationships, Pakistan will continue to provide logistic support, safe havens and sanctuaries to terrorists in Kashmir.

REFERENCES

1. It is believed that Kashyap Rishi laid the foundation of the state and hence the state is named after him (Nilmat Puran). For details see Koumidi, *Kashmir: Its Cultural Heritage* (Bombay: Asia Publishing House, 1952).
2. Premnath Bazaz, *The History of Struggle for Freedom in Kashmir* (new Delhi: Kashmir Publishing Co. 1954), pp. 5-6.
3. V.P. Menon, *Integration of Indian States* (Bombay: Oriesst Longman,

1961).
4. M.S. Deora and R.G. Grover (ed.), *Documents on Kashmir Problems*, Vol. I (New Delhi: Discovery Publishing House, 1991), p.10.
5. Gopalswami Ayyangar, *UN Security Council Official Records*, Third Year, 226th-240th meeting 5-4th Feb, 1948 (New York; Lake Success: UNSC, 1948), p.14.
6. UNSCOR (New York, Lake Success: UNSC, 1988, Third Year 226-240 meeting 6th Jan-4th Feb, 1948) p. 14.
7. B.M. Kaul, *Confrontation with Pakistan* (Delhi: Vikas Publication, 1971) pp.6-12.
8. Sisir Gupta, *Kashmir: A Study in India-Pakistan Relations* (Bombay: Asia Publishing House, 1966), p.108.
9. Lord Birdwood, *Two Nations and Kashmir* (London: Rober Hale, 1956), pp.53-6.
10. V.P. Menon, *Integration of Indian States*, op.cit., p.384.
11. Ibid, p.377.
12. Russel Brines, *The Indo-Pakistan Conflict* (London: Pall Mall Press, 1968), p.78. Also see M.C Chagta, *Kashmir, 1947-65* (New Delhi: Publication Division, 1965).
13. For details, see S.M. Bark, *Pakistan's Foreign Policy* (London: Oxford University Press, 1973).
14. Keith Colland, *Pakistan: A Political Study* (London: Allen and Unwin, 1957), p.15.
15. Z.A Bhutto, *The Myth of Independence* (London: Oxford University Press, 1969), p.113.
16. Indira Gandhi, *Lok Sabha Debates*, Vol. X (New Delhi: Lok Sabha Secretariat, 17th December, 1971), pp.69-71.
17. Stephen P; Cohen, *Security of South Asia* (New Delhi: Vistar Publication, 1987), p.230.
18. Sisir Gupta, *Kashmir: A Study in India Pakistan Relations*, op.cit., p.15.
19. G.M. Myed, quoted in Syed Ziaullahigad Samuel Baid, *Pakistan: An End without Beginning* (New Delhi: Lancer International, 1985), p.5.
20. Stephen P. Cohen, *The Pakistan Army* (New Delhi: Himalayan Books, 1984), p.108.
21. Religion is matter of faith which cannot be switched off because there is erosion of its relevance in changing society. It does not aim to achieve socio-economic problems. It's aim is spiritual awakening and provides guidelines for moral values in social life. It could be interpreted according to changing situation. But cannot be rejected in the same way as an ideology could be.
22. Arif Hussain, *Pakistan: Its Ideology and Foreign Policy* (London: France Cass and Co., 1966), p.XVI.
23. Karan Singh, "Future of Kashmir", *Times of India* (Bombay), 31 August 1992, p.10.
24. In personal interview with JKLF militants, and also *Times of India* (Bombay), 12 January 1992, p.7.
25. George Joseph, *Indian Express* (Bombay), 18 July 1992, p.7.
26. *Indian Express* (Bombay), 1 March 1992.

27. *India Today* (New Delhi), 31 December 1992, pp.100-1.
28. G.M. Telang, "The Kashmir Issues", *Indian Express* (Bombay), 29 February 1992, p. 8.
29. Jagmohan, *My Frozen Turbulence in Kashmir*, op.cit., p.140.
30. B.H. Kaul, *The Untold Story* (Bombay: Allied Publishers, 1967), p.102.
31. P.M. Kaul Banzai, *Kashmir and Power Politics* (Delhi: Metropolitan-Books, 1966), p. 97.
32. *India Year Book: A Reference Annual* (New Delhi: Publication Division, Government of India, 1981), p.441.
33. B.M. Kaul, *Confrontation with Pakistan*, op.cit., p. 113.
34. Ibid, p. 23.
35. Ibid, p. 113.
36. Ibid. p. 23-24.
37. General Mohammad Musa, *My Version: India Pakistan War, 1965* (Lahore: Wazadali Ltd., 1983), pp. 2-3.
38. B.M. Kaul, *The Untold Story*, op.cit., p.743.
39. K.P. Candeth, *The Western Front: The Indo-Pak War, 1971* (New Delhi: Allied Publishers, 1984), p.64.
40. Ibid, p.37.
41. Ibid.
42. Ibid.
43. Stanley Wolpert, *Roots of Confrontation in South Asia* (New York: Oxford University Press, 1982), p.117.
44. Security Council Official Records, Documents S/628. (Third Year Supplement for November1948), pp.139-144.
45. UNSCOR, 3rd Year, No. 1-15, 226th to 240th Meeting, 6th January-4th February, 1948 (New York: The United Nations, 1948), pp.285-286.
46. Ibid.
47. Ibid., p.296.
48. L.P. Sen, *Slender was the Thread* (New Delhi: Sangam Books, 1973), pp.101-104.
49. UNSCOR, 32, 1950, Supplement for September-December, 1950), pp.36-47.
50. Michael Brecher, *The Struggle for Kashmir* (New York: Oxford University Press, 1953), p.34.
51. Sir Claude Anchenleck qtd. Stanley Wolpert, *In Roots of Confrontation in South Asia*.
52. Jawaharlal Nehru, *Lok Sabha Debates*, Part II, 12th session, 1956, 29th March, 1956, (New Delhi: Lok Sabha Secretariat, 1956), p.3734.
53. Qtd. in P.N. Dhar, "The Kashmir Problem: Political and Economic Background" *India Quarterly*, Vol. VII, No. 62 (New Delhi: 1951), p.310.
54. A. Appadorai, *Documents on India's Foreign Policy, 1947-72*, Vol. I, (New Delhi: Oxford University Press, 1982), p.279.
55. S.S. Bindra, *Indo-Pakistan Relations: Tashkent to Shimla* (New Delhi: Deep and Deep, 1981), p. 216.
56. Ibid., p. 214.
57. G.S. Bhargava, *Crush India – Gen. Yaheya Khan, or Pakistan's Death Wish* (Delhi: ISSD Publication, 1972) p. 47.

58. Kenneth Galbraith, *Ambassadors Journal* (Bombay: Jaico Publishing, 1972), p.167.
59. *Keesingh's Contemporary Archives*, Vol. VIII. June-July, 19520, p.11198.
60. K.P. Mishra, *Kashmir and India's Foreign Policy* (Allahabad: Chugh Publication, 1979), p.38.
61. Ibid., p. 337.
62. Attar Chand, *IslamicNations and Kashmir Problem* (Delhi: Raj Publications, 1994), pp.40-41.
63. Lord Birdwood, *Two Nations and Kiashmir*, op.cit., pp.53-56.
64. K. Subrahmanyam, *Indian Security Perspective* (New Delhi: ABC Publishing, 1982), p.147.
65. Jagmohan, *My Frozen Turbulence in Kashmir*, op.cit., p.425.
66. Ibid., pp.406-410.
67. Ibid., p.406.
68. Terrorist Activities Disruptive Act (TADA) came into existence in 1985. But the statistics under TADA could be made available only in 1988. Crimes unlikely to be associated with Pak. Sponsored terrorism have been excluded from different heads of crimes in the chart.
69. Attar Chand, *Pakistan Terrorism in Punjab and Kashmir* (Delhi: Amar Prakashan, 1991), p.117.
70. Afsir Karim, *Counter-Terrorism*, op.cit., p.117.
71. *The Times of India* (Bombay), 15 December 1991.
72. *Indian Express* (Bombay), 5 October 1991.
73. K. Doraiswamy, in personal interview with the author.
74. Afsir Karim, *Counter Terrorism*, op.cit., p. 49.
75. *Indian Express* (Bombay), 29 October 1991.
76. Afsir Karim, op.cit., p.49.
77. Rajesh Kadian, *The Kashmir Triangle* (New Delhi: Vision Books, 1992).
78. *Census of India*, Jammu and Kashmir, Part V and A and B, Migration Table, pp.11-37 (New Delhi: Publication Division, 1981).
79. *Indian Express* (Bombay), 25 April 1993, p.3.
80. *Indian Express* (Bombay), 18 July 1992, p.7.

Chapter 6

Conclusion

There are several instruments used by nation-states to achieve foreign policy objectives in international relations. Diplomacy, propaganda, international law, international organizations, foreign aid and war have come to exist as regular instruments through which nation-states realize their foreign policy goals. The efficacy of each of these instruments, as mentioned in the first chapter, has evolved in the course of time in response to conditions in international politics. While war and diplomacy are ancient instruments, others are products of the post-World War II international scenario. The establishment of the UN, the first international organization of its kind, is an example of the post-World War II situation. The major powers of the world realized the need for an international body to solve problems caused by war as well as to maintain peaceful co-existence of nation-states. Hence, the UN came into existence. In similar circumstances international law, propaganda and foreign assistance were accepted as instrument to accomplish foreign policy goals of a nation.

Normally, a nation-state uses one or the other of these instruments to achieve its foreign policy goals. If the employed instrument fails to achieve foreign policy goals; an alternative instrument is adopted. But when one of these instruments works nations tend to adopt unconventional means to achieve their foreign policy objectives. The use of terrorism is one of the unconventional means that has now become recognized in international relations. It has emerged as an alarming addition to the ever-growing list of foreign policy instruments.

The nature of terrorism is such that no nation or political movement would opt for its use unless it is desperate to settle certain vital issues. This is precisely because the very concept of terrorism is controversial. Scholars all over the world have interpreted it according to their own context and understanding of the phenomenon. At times their opinions are so divided that one person's terrorist becomes another's freedom fighter. But in spite of all the differences that exist in the definition of terrorism, there are certain characteristics that are common to all the interpretations. We must admit that differences always exist in every concept. If we keep pointing out differences only, there will be no conclusion or solution to the problem. Therefore, my effort has been to analyze different positions in such a way that a working definition of terrorism is evolved. The conceptual understanding of terrorism is important because, without proper understanding and a clear definition it will be difficult to understand its application in international politics.

The role of terrorism in international relations has become such a common phenomenon in the post-World War II period that often terrorism is defined as international or transnational terrorism. This is mainly because, as we have learned from the September 11, 2001 attacks that leveled the World Trade Center (WTC) in New York and damaged the Pentagon in Washington DC, terrorists cannot operate without international support that comes directly or indirectly from both government and private terrorist organizations. The support of private organizations, however, is not always as alarming as the one that comes from government agencies. The resources of a government are often required for terrorists to operate in the supposedly hostile country. Terrorism sponsored by a government can be carried on until the foreign policy goals of the sponsoring nation in achieve. It is this government support for terrorism in international relations that makes this phenomenon alarming to humankind and poses a threat to the territorial security of nation-states. Yet not many substantial works have been conducted to analyze circumstances under which a nation uses terrorism and what the underlying causes for its application are. Instead, political leaders of nation-states are involved in accusing one another of sponsoring terrorism. But the point is not who used it first, but to accept the fact that every nation uses terrorism to achieve foreign policy goals at different points of time in their national history.

This study conducted before the New York attacks and the ensuing "war on terrorism" by the Bush Administration, has examined the use of terrorism by the government of Pakistan in relation with India as a vivid example. Pakistan has been using terror tactics in Punjab and Jammu and Kashmir to achieve its foreign policy objectives which is the creation of a sovereign Sikh state and the conquest of Kashmir respectively. Pakistani leaders first attempted to achieve these goals through normal instruments of foreign policy. But when these efforts proved futile, the Pakistan government switched over to the use of terrorism in a well-planned manner, which created a tumultuous uproar in the body politic of India.

The impact of Pak-sponsored terrorism on India is tragic. Prime Minister Indira Gandhi, was assassinated on October 31, 1984 by aspirants of Khalistan and the spate of violence and terrorism that followed her death made it clear that India was under terrorist siege. The foreign policy designs of Pakistan were exposed forcing the government of India to come up with quick counter-terrorism action plans and programs. The enactment of TADA (now scraped), NDPS (Narcotic Drug and Psychotic Substance) and numerous other acts that came into enforcement in Punjab and Jammu and Kashmir during this period are manifestations of the threat India felt from Pakistan's use of terrorism as an instrument of foreign policy.

Therefore, in the case of Indo-Pak relations, three observations are clear. First, terrorism, has emerged as an instrument to achieve the foreign policy goals of nation-states. Second, terrorism is used when normal instruments of foreign policy fail to fulfill aspirations of a nation. Third, the extensive use of terrorism by Pakistan proves partial efficacy of terrorism in international relations.

THE U.S. AND GLOBAL TERRORISM

The end of the Cold War and the disintegration of the former Soviet Union created a new wave of thinking. With the collapse of the Eastern European Communist empire, it was believed that terrorism would also diminish from international politics. But, it did not. As a matter of fact, there is a new wave of international terrorism in the new world order.

With the end of the Cold War, the U.S. had achieved its

foreign policy goal to become the only superpower, but countries that enjoyed the patronage of either of the two superpowers, are left in uncertainty and despair. The disintegration of the former Soviet Union has left a vacuum in the power politics of the world. So in the post-Cold War situation, every nation is desperate to explore its status in the emerging new world order, for, they have either lost or about to loose the umbrella of superpower protection. For instance, Syria and Libya, which constantly received assistance from the USSR government, cannot depend on Russia anymore. Russia has lost its superpower status and the country is yet to overcome the post-disintegration politico-economic crisis. The end of the Cold War and the U.S. dominance over world politics give clear indication that developing countries cannot afford overt war as a means to achieve their goals. The case of Iraq's venture in Kuwait in 1991 substantiates this argument. Saddam Hussein decided to settle territorial disputes between Iraq and Kuwait through overt aggression without analyzing the repercussions. This action by Iraq made the U.S. intervention inevitable. The U.S. along with its allies obtained UN sanctions to wage war on Iraq.

It may have been this war that triggered the new wave of terrorism that culminated in the September attacks on the U.S. During the war waged on Iraq by the U.S. and its allies, Saddam Hussein used the rhetoric of "Islam in danger" to mobilize Arab opinion against the war. In many radio broadcasts, he urged Muslims worldwide to inflict terrorism against the forces of evil.[1] The motivation to attack U.S. interests in East Africa, in the Middle East and in the U.S. itself goes back to some of these calls by Hussein. Americans do not always understands that.

Supremacy of the U.S. in global politics is a cause for concern to the international community. Weaker nations are concerned by U.S. intervention all over the world. There is a fear psychosis of being contained by the only superpower if they do not toe the U.S. line and approach. Libya, Iraq, Yugoslavia and now Afghanistan have had to bear the brunt of U.S. power. This situation has created an obsession among nations that failure to respect U.S. interests triggers punitive and coercive measures to teach them a lesson. Thus there exists perpetual fear among nations that might inspire the use of terrorism against U.S. interests to resolve international disputes (i.e. the Arab-Israeli conflict) or to revenge prior international actions by the U.S. (such as the attacks on the World Trade Center and the Pentagon).

TERRORISM IN AFGHANISTAN

The U.S. equipped Afghan Mujahideens with sophisticated weapons to fight against the Soviet Union without analyzing the fact that after the withdrawal of the Soviet army, these extremists could be used to foment trouble in the region and around the world. Existing political conditions in Afghanistan, Jammu and Kashmir in India and the Central Asian Republics are a result of this miscalculation.

The Mujahideens were armed and well equipped to carry acts of subversion and terrorism for the next two decades if left undeterred. The rise of the Taliban and the infighting among different heterogeneous groups in Afghanistan is an example of the grim situation the country is passing through. Afghanistan has become a land of militancy from where militants are created and trained to cross any frontier for abetting terrorism. Until recently, these heavily armed Mujahideens were being used by Pakistan to sponsor terrorism in Jammu and Kashmir in India.

TERRORISM AND FOREIGN POLICY

The decision makers' approach towards the application of terrorism is hypocritical. This hypocrisy is mainly because no nation—not even the U.S.—has accepted that terrorism has emerged as an instrument to achieve certain foreign policy goals. U.S. policy analysts still oppose it from a moral perspective. But if analyzed from a narrower perspective like this, even war could be considered immoral and thus not acceptable as an instrument in international relations. In fact, in the early phases even war was not an acceptable means. Questions like just and unjust war were raised and debated. In 1928, the Kellog-Briand Pact declared war illegal.[2] But nation-states have used war to achieve foreign policy goals. Today even international organizations such as the UN have no inhibitions in granting permission to declare war be it for just or unjust causes as an acceptable instrument.

In the same way, it could be argued that terrorism should also be recognized as an instrument to achieve foreign policy goals. The justification for its use could be argued separately. But its application by nations is not be denied and if we accept that terrorism has come to exist as an instrument to achieve foreign policy objectives, it would be feasible to formulate rules to govern its application. Once it is established as an acceptable instrument, and certain conditions are attached to it, the nation-states may restrain from abetting terrorism to achieve their objectives in the same way that they avoid going to war.

PREVENTION OF TERRORISM

Prevention of terrorism is an important issue in international relations. Until recently the scope of state-sponsored terrorism has been limited to regional conflicts in bilateral relations. But, after the attacks on the U.S. its growth has become obvious. In the future it is possible that nations having an identical world perspective, ideology or religion could get together and use terrorism in pursuance of their goals. This could broaden the scope of terrorism to the multilateral level. Thus, if international security and peaceful co-existence is to be maintained, the use of terrorism by states has to be curbed.

One of the most convenient ways to curb state-sponsored terrorism is to utilize international forums. The UN, being the highest body in the international system, obviously is the place to start. The good offices of the UN could be used to pressurize states sponsoring terrorism.

The importance of the UN to curbing state-sponsored terrorism was well expressed by the former Secretary General of the UN, Kurt Waldheim, who, while referring to conflict and violence around the world, stated that "a number of key disputes are dangerously interconnected with the world peace, which remain unresolved and continue to give rise to violence and frustration, and various other forms of terrorism have taken an increasing toll." He further emphasized that "timely concerted steps should be taken to deal with them effectively before they grow out of control."[3]

Way back in 1973, the UN did realize the need to control

the growth of terrorism in international relations. An ad-hoc committee was set up and a definition of the term, terrorism, was discussed at length. But there existed such a wide gap of interpretation among member nations that they could not come to an agreement on the definition of terrorism[4] let alone agree on measures to curb it. The failure to reach an agreement on definition, however, did not dissuade member nations to recognize the problem and adopt policies to curb state-sponsored terrorism. There is problem in defining terrorism, but it is easy to identify, and on the basis of identity itself, certain policy could be adopted to restrain use of terrorism in international relations.

The UN has already discussed state-sponsored terrorism extensively. In 1987, it adopted a resolution condemning all acts of terrorism as criminal and innumerable measures were suggested for its prevention. Similarly, the UN can verify facts on file from different sources and decide whether a particular nation is using terrorism as an instrument to achieve foreign policy goals or not; and to what extent is their involvement and what punitive action could be taken to dissuade nation-states from its application.

This is not an uphill task. The UN has discussed and adopted resolutions on various issues related to international security. The UN has also given overwhelming support to the U.S. since the September 11, 2001 attacks. But more importantly, efforts have to be made to analyze the causes and ramifications for the use of terrorism by member nations.

United Nations
Meanwhile, the UN has to acknowledge that state-sponsored terrorism is not a regional phenomenon that can be dealt at the bilateral level. Rather, it is a global phenomenon that needs UN intervention to curb at the global level.

A proposal for a compulsory extradition treaty among UN members would be very useful in checking the growth of terrorism in international relations. The absence of an extradition treaty among nations jeopardizes efforts of the victim state to eliminate and prevent terrorism. Terrorists, be they sponsored by states or individual groups, are highly mobile. They are quick in crossing boundaries into safe havens, where they cannot be sent back unless the nations concerned have extradition treaty with each other.

So far extradition treaties comes under the sphere of bilateral negotiations. So far no action has been taken to make it an issue of global concern. This situation is favorable for terrorists as they can escape to countries which do not have extradition with the victim nation. The refusal by Afghanistan to hand over Osama Bin Laden is a case in point.

This escape route, however, could be checked if the UN makes extradition compulsory among the member nations. It is not a difficult task because the basic aim of extradition is prevention of crime, which most of the nations would agree to abide by. Compulsory extradition would restrain activities of terrorists, because they would be inconstant fear of being caught, and sent back for trial; and ultimately would be punished for their terrorist activities.

Pressure Tactics at the UN
The UN can also be a forum where political and economic pressure is put on countries involved in abetting terrorism. The UN, as the largest body involved in the overall economic development of the member nations can pressure smaller states not to support terrorism. The International Monetary Fund (IMF) and the World Bank are the two major financing institutions that monitor economic growth of developing countries. These prime institutions could be used to pursue the realization of this goal. By maintaining or controlling financial flow to the different countries, these institutions are in a position to put pressure on states sponsoring terrorism.

Terrorism Prevention in India
While on one hand, terrorism is on the rise in South Asia, on the other hand, nuclearization of India and Pakistan has restrained them from waging a declared war. The nuclear test conducted by both India and Pakistan in May 1998 has raised the alarm of mutual destruction. Hence instead of using total war, Pakistan has switched over to application of limited war and terrorism to achieve its foreign policy goal in India. The limited war in Kargil and Drass sectors in Kashmir in 1999 and the incursions during U.S. attacks on Afghanistan substantiate

this argument.

To counter-act future Pak-sponsored terrorism, India must understand that terrorism passes through various phases. Each of these phases needs to be counter-acted separately and according to the situation.

The first is political phase. A terrorist group may come into being as a political party or movement in the beginning. They participate in the political process of the country, and when they fail to achieve their goals either because of lack of popular support, ideological loopholes, corruption or malpractices in the process of electioneering, they may adopt a path of violence and open confrontation with the government concerned. This phase is the beginning of terrorism. At this phase, terrorist groups are not fully equipped with arms and infrastructure facilities, nor are they trained in the application of weapons. They are novices at this stage of their struggle. If a government adopts preventative measures to keep watch over the activities of the members of the disgruntled political parties and their changing political aspirations, it is possible that the growth of terrorism could be restrained. The All India Sikh Students Federation (AISSF) in Punjab could be given as an example of the same situation. The case of the JKLF in Jammu and Kashmir is another case of shifting aspirations of political parties from active politics to violence and subversion.

The second phase of terrorism is active participation of terrorists in violence and subversive activities. At this stage terrorism has to be curbed at the administrative level by adopting a policy of deterrence and by the implementation of such plans as a special task forces of police and intelligence departments to deal with the situation. This has been practiced by the U.S. government on a very large scale. Delta Force and FBI's Hostage Rescue Team (HRT) are examples of the U.S. counter-terrorism measures.[5] In the same rein, India too, can opt for a special task force to combat terrorism. Legislation like Terrorist Activities Disruptive Act (TADA), which came into existence in 1985 (now scraped), could be considered as another step towards the same. But such legislation, at times, becomes the subject of severe criticism for being misused by the government to contain opposition parties. This hampers the process of combating terrorism, especially in a pluralist democratic society like India. In order to avoid this, the government of India has now set up an independent permanent National Security Council (NSC) which is devoid of political affiliation and patronage. Under the auspices of the NSC, a special task force could be created when required and dismantled once the goal is realized. In addition, the government of India should create an operation task force from within the military in cooperation with the intelligence services and the police to flush out terrorists and the stockpile of arms and ammunition. Military action, without having tried the police first, is counter-productive in so far as terrorism is concerned. First, because is shows apathy of the government towards grievances of the people and second, because it shows an excessive use of force and violence by the military to deal with a crisis which could be controlled by the police.

To sum it up, India must be prepared to fight terrorism at phase one and also at the second phase. And, just as the U.S. has prepared itself for a long and bitter war against terrorism, so should India and all peace-loving nations.

REFERENCES

1. *Indian Express* (Bombay), January 23, 1991, p. 14.
2. Louis Delvet, *The United Nations* (London: Phoenix House, 1946), p.11.
3. *Annual Review of United Nations Affairs*, compiled and edited by William A. Landskron (New York: Oceana Publications, 1983), p.3.
4. United Nations, *Report of the Ad-hoc Committee on International Terrorism*, General Assembly Official Records, 28th Session, Supplement No. 28, A/9028 (New York: United Nations, 1973).
5. Karl Sager, *The Anti-terrorism Handbook*, op.cit., pp.29-30.

Bibliography

PRIMARY SOURCES

Census of India, *Punjab*, Vol. VI (Shimla: Government of India Press, 1941).

—, *Jammu and Kashmir*, Part XII, Series- 8 (Srinagar: Directorate of Census Operation, 1981).

Crime in India (New Delhi: National Crime Record Bureau, 1980 to 1990).

India Year Book (New Delhi: Publication Division, Government of India, 1981).

Lok Sabha Debates (New Delhi: Lok Sabha Secretariat, 1956 and 1971).

Marcquess of Linlithgow, Private and Personal Letters, MSS. EUR. F. 125/11 (New Delhi: Viceroy's House,1942).

Ministry of External Affairs, *Annual Report, 1990-91* (New Delhi: Government of India, 1991).

Ministry of Home Affairs, *Annual Report, 1989-90* (New Delhi: Government of India, 1990).

Office of the Director-General of Police, Intelligence, *Monthly Terrorist Review on Punjab*, Copy No.22, Secret, (Chandigarh: May, 1993).

SAARC Regional Convention on Suppression of Terrorism (Kathmandu: SAARC Secretariat, 4th November, 1987).

Statistical Abstract of the U.S. (Washington D.C.: US Department of Commerce, Bureau of the Census, 1992).

Terrorist Activities Disruptive Act (TADA) (New Delhi: Government of India, 1985).

United Nations, General Assembly, Thirty Ninth Session Agenda, Item – 143, Resolution Adopted by the General Assembly, (On the Report of the First Committee, A/39/761).

United Nations, Report of the Ad-Hoc Committee on International Terrorism, General Assembly Official Records: Twenty Eighth Session Supplement No.28, A/9028, (New York: United Nations, 1973).

UN High Commission for Refugees, A/AC, 96/677.

United Nations Security Council Resolution, (UNSCR) S/3821, 1949.

UNSCOR, Third Year, 226th-240th Meeting, 6th January-14th February, 1948.

UNSCOR, 32, 1950 Supplement for September-Decembet, 1950. United Nations Secretariat Study, Note 1, Annexe, 1 at 1, Text of the 1937 Convention for the Prevention and Punishment of Terrorism, Note 2, Appendix 1 at 196 (New York: UN Secretariat).

United Nations Economic and Social Council, Ad-Hoc Committee on Genocide, Report to the Economic and Social Council on the meetings of the Committee held at Lake Success, 5th April to 10th May, 1948.

UNSCOR, Twenty Seventh Year, Supplement for April, May and June, Document S/10705, (New York: United Nations, 1972).

White Paper on Punjab Agitation, (New Delhi: Government of India, 10th July, 1984).

SECONDARY SOURCES

BOOKS

Akbar, M.J., Kashmir: Behind the Veil (Delhi: Penguin Books, 1991).

—, India: The Siege Within, Challenges to a Nation's Unity (Middlesex: Penguin Books, 1985).

Akhtar, Jamna Das, Pak Espionage in India (Delhi: Oriental Publishers, 1971).

Alexander, Yonah, International Terrorism: National, Regional and Global Perspectives (New York: Praeger Publishers, 1976).

—, Carlton, David and Wilkinson, Paul, Terrorism: Theory and Practice (Colorado: Westviews Press, 1979).

— and Finger, Seymour, M., Terrorism: Interdisciplinary Perspectives (New York: The John Jay Press, 1977).

Alexander, Yonah, and Friedlander, Robert, *Self-Determination: National, Regional and Global Dimensions* (Colorado: Westviews Press, 1979).

Ali, Tariq, *Pakistan: Military Rule or People's Power* (London: Jonathan Cape, 1970).

—, *Can Pakistan Survive?* (Middlesex: Penguin Books, 1983).

Andies, Helmut, *Rule of Terror: Russia Under Lenin and Stalin* (New York: Rinehart and Winston, 1969).

Ansari, Shaukatullah, *Pakistan: The Problem of India* (Lahore: Minerva Book Shop, 1944).

Appadorai, A., *Documents on India's Foreign Policy, 1947-72* (Delhi: Oxford University Press, 1982).

Arendt, Hannah, *On Violence* (New York: Harcourt Brace and World Inc., 1969).

Aron, Raymond, *Peace and War* (London: Weidenfield and Nicolson, 1962).

—, *On War* (London: Secker and Warburg, 1958).

Bajpai, U.S., *India's Security: The Politico Strategic Environment* (New Delhi: Lancer Publishers, 1983).

Bamzai, Prithvi Nath Kaul, *Kashmir and Power Politics* (Delhi: Metropolitan Book Co., 1966).

Bassiouni, M. Cherif, *International Terrorism and Political Crimes* (Illinois: Charles C. Thomas, 1975).

Bazaz, Prem Nath, *Kashmir in Crucible* (New Delhi: Pamposh Publications, 1967).

—, *The History of Struggle for Freedom in Kashmir* (New Delhi: Kashmir Publishing Co., 1954).

Bell, J. and Bowyer, A. *Time of Terror: How Democratic Societies Respond to Revolutionary Violence* (New York: Basic Books, 1978).

Bhargava, G.S., *Crush India* (Delhi: ISSD Publication, 1972).

Bhutto, Z. A., *The Myth of Independence* (London: Oxford University Press, 1969).

Bienen, Henry, *Violence and Social Change: A Review of Current Literature* (Chicago: University of Chicago Press, 1968).

Bindra, S. S., *India Pakistan Relations* (New Delhi: Deep and Deep, 1981).

Birdwood, Lord, *Two Nations and Kashmir* (London: Robert Hale, 1956).

Bocca, Geoffrey, *The Secret Army* (New Jersey: Prentice Hall, 1968).

Brandt, Willy, *North-South Dialogue* (London: Pan Book Ltd., 1980).

Brecher, Michael, *The Struggle for Kashmir* (New York: Oxford University Press, 1953).

Brines, Russel, *The Indo-Pakistan Conflict* (London: Pall Mall Press, 1968).

Brink, Jan Ten and Hedeman J., *Robespierre and the Red Terror* (London: Hutchinson and Co., 1899).

Burke, S. M., *Pakistan's Foreign Policy: An Historical Analysis* (London: Oxford University Press, 1973).

—, *Mainsprings of Indian and Pakistani Foreign Policy* (Karachi: Oxford University Press, 1975).

Candeth, K. P., *The Western Front: The Indo-Pak War, 1971* (New Delhi: Allied Publishers, 1984).

Carlton, David S. and Schaerif, Carlo, *International Terrorism and World Security* (London: Cromhelm, 1975).

Carr, E. H., *Studies in Revolution* (New York: Grosset and Dulop, 1964).

Centril, Hadley, *The Politics of Despair* (New York: Basic Books Inc., 1958).

Chand, Attar, *Islamic Nations and Kashmir Problem* (Delhi: Raj Publications, 1994).

—, *Pakistan Terrorism in Punjab and Kashmir* (Delhi: Amar Prakashan, 1991).

Chagla, M. C., *Kashmir , 1947-1965* (New Delhi: Publication Division, 1965).

Chopra, V. D. et al., *Agony of Punjab* (New Delhi: Patriot Publishers, 1984).

Claude, Inis, L. Jr., *Power and International Relations* (New York: Random House, 1962).

Clines, Ray S. and Alexander, *Terrorism as State Sponsored Covert Warfare* (Virginia: Hero Books, 1986).

Clutterbuck, Richard, *Living with Terrorism* (New Rochellc: Arlington House, 1975).

—, *Guerrillas and Terrorists* (London: Faber and Faber , 1977).

Cohen, Stephen, P., *Security of South Asia* (New Delhi: Vistar Publications, 1987).

—, *The Pakistan Army* (New Delhi: Himalayan Books, 1984).

Collard, Keith, *Pakistan: A Political Study* (London: George Allen & Unwin, 1957).

—, *Pakistan's Foreign Policy* (Hongkong: Hongkong University Press, 1959).

Cranston, Maurice W., *The New Left* (New York: The Library Press, 1971).

Crozier, Brian, *The Rebels: A Study of Post-War Insurrection* (London: Chetto and Windus, 1960).

Cunningham, Joseh Davey, *A History of the Sikhs* (London: John Murray, 1849).

Dang, Satyapal, *Genesis of Terrorism: An Analytical Study of Punjab Terrorists* (New Delhi: Patriot Publishers, 1988).

Dasgupta, Jyoti Bhushan, *Indo-Pakistan Relations, 1947-1955* (Amsterdam: Djambatan, 1958).

Davis, Angela, *An Autobiography* (New York: Random House, 1947).

Deora, M. S. and Grover, R., *Documents on Kashmir Problem* (New Delhi: Discovery Publishing House, 1991).

Dobson, Christopher, *The Carlos Complex: A Study in Terror* (New York: Putman's Sons, 1977).

—, and Payne, Ronald, *The Terrorists: Their Weapons, Leadersand Tactics* (New York: Facts on File, 1979).

Dror, Y., *Crazy States* (New York: Millwood, 1980).

Fanon, Frantz, *Wretched of the Earth* (New York: Grove Press, 1967).

Fieldman, Herbert, *The End and the Beginning, Pakistan – 1969-1974* (London: Oxford University Press, 1975).

Frankel, Joseph, *The Making of Foreign Policy* (New York: Oxford University Press, 1963).

Friedlander, Robert A., *Terrorism: Documents of International and Local Control* (New York: Oceana Publication,1979).

Galbraith, Kenneth, *Ambassador's Journal* (Bombay: Jaico Publishing, 1972).

Gaucher, Roland, *The Terrorists: From Tsarist Russia to the OAS* (London: Secker and Warburg, 1968).

Gendzier, Irene, L., *Frantz Fanon: A Critical Study* (New York: Pantheon Books, 1973).

Goldwin, Robert A., *Why Foreign Aid* (Chicago: Rand McNally & Co., 1968).

Gouba, K. L., *Pakistan Today* (Bombay: Thakkar & Co., 1976).

Gour, H. S., *The Hindu Code* (Nagpur).

Green, G., *Terrorism: Is It Revolutionary?* (New York: New Outlook Publications, 1970).

Green, Leslie C., *Nature and Control of International Terrorism* (Alberta: University of Alberta, 1974).

Gregory, Frank and Palmer, Joseph, *Ten Years of Terrorism* (New York: Crane Russak Co., 1979).

Gribble, Leonard, *Hands of Terror* (London: Frederick Muller Ltd., 1960).

Grosscu, Bean, *The Explosion of Terrorism* (New York: Macmillan, 1987).

Gupta, Jyoti Sen, *History of Freedom Movement in Bangladesh* (Calcutta: Noya Prakashan, 1974).

Gupta, Sisir, *Kashmir: A Study of India-Pakistan Relations* (Bombay: Asia Publishing House, 1966).

Gurr, *Ted Robert, Why Men Rebel?* (New Jersey: Princeton University Press, 1970).

Hacker, Frederick J., *Crusader, Criminals, Crazies: Terror and Terrorism in Our Time* (New York: Bantam Books, 1978).

Hass, Ernest B. and Whitting S. Allen, *Dynamics of International Relations* (New York: McGraw Hill Book, 1949).

Hoffman, P., *Peace Can be Won* (New York: Doubleday, 1951).

Holsti, K.J., *Internatinal Politics* (New Delhi: Prentice Hall India Ltd., 1978).

Hussain, Arif, *Pakistan: Its Ideology and Foreign Policy* (London: Frank Cass & Co. Ltd., 1966).

Jagmohan, *My Frozen Turbulence in Kashmir* (New Delhi: Allied Publishers, 1991).

Jenkins, Brian M., *Terrorism and Kidnapping* (Santa Monica: Rand Corporation, June 1974).

—, *New Modes of Conflict* (Santa Monica: Rand Corporation, 34th Year).

Johnson, Chalmers, *Perspectives of Terrorism* (Berkley: University of California, 1979).

Joshi, Chand, *Bhindranwale: Myth and Reality* (New Delhi: Vikas

Publishing House, 1984).

Kadian, Rajesh, *The Kashmir Tangle* (New Delhi: Vision Books, 1992).

Kamath, P. M., *Foreign Policy Making and International Politics* (New Delhi: Radiant Publishers, 1990).

Karim, Afsir, Maj. Gen. (AVSM Rtd.), *Counter Terrorism: The Pakistan Factor* (New Delhi: Lancer International, 1991).

Kaul, Lt. Gen. B. M., *The Untold Story* (Bombay: Allied Publishers, 1967).

—, *Confrontation With Pakistan* (Delhi: Vikas Publication, 971).

Keohane, Robert and Nye, Joseph S., *Transnational Relations in World Politics* (Cambridge: Harvard University Press, 1973).

Kim, Young Hum, *The CIA* (Massachussetts: D.C. Health and Co. 1968).

Korbel, Joseph, *Danger in Kashmir* (New Jersey: Princeton University Press, 1954).

Koumidi, *Kashmir: Its Cultural Heritage* (Bombay: Asia Publishing House, 1952).

Krishnarao, K. V., *Prepare or Perish* (New Delhi: Lancer International, 1991).

Kulkarni, V. B., *Pakistan: Its Origin and Relations With India* (New Delhi: Sterling Publishers, 1988).

Labrousse, Allain, *The Tupamaros* (Middlesex: Penguin Books, 1973).

Lacquer, Walter, *The Terrorism Reader: A Historical Anthology* (New York: New American Library, 1978).

—, *Terrorism* (Boston: Little Brown and Co., 1977).

—, *The Age of Terror* (London: Wiedenfield and Nicolson, 1987).

Lakhanpal, P. L., *Kashmir Conspiracy Case* (Delhi: International Publications, 1959).

Lester, A., *Political Terroirism* (New York: Facts on File, 1975).

Livingstone, Neil C., *The War Against Terrorism* (Massachusetts: D. C. Health Co., 1982).

—, and Terrell, E. Arnold, *Fighting Back* (Massachusetts: D.C. Health Co., 1984).

Lombart, Richard S., *Propoganda* (London: Thomas Nelson & Sons, 1939).

Lovell, John P., *Foreign Policy in Perspective* (New York: Richard

Winstone, Inc., 1970).

Macridis, Roy C., *Foreign Policy in World Politics* (New Jersey: Englewood Cliffs, 1958).

Marcuse, Herbert, *An Essay on Liberation* (Boston: Beacon Press, 1969).

MuCuen, John J., *The Art of Counter Revolutionary War, The Strategy of Counter Insurgency* (London: Faber and Faber, 1966).

McClure, Brooks, *The Dynamics of Terrorism* (Gaithersburg: International Association of Chiefs of Police, 1976).

McKnight, Gerald, *The Terrorist Mind: Why They Hijack, Kidnap, Bomb and Kill?* (Indianpolis: The Bobbs Merrill Co., 1974).

Menon, V. P., *The Story of the Integration of the Indian States* (Bombay: Orient Longman, 1961).

Merkl, Peter H., *Political Violence and Terror: Motifs and Motivations* (California: University of California Press, 1986).

Mishra, K.P., *Kashmir and India's Foreign Policy* (Allahabad: Chugh Publication, 1979).

Montgomery, John D., *Foreign Aid in International Politics* (Bombay: Allied Publisher, 1969).

Morgenthou, Hans J., *Politics Among Nations* (New York: Alfred K. Knopf, 1950).

—, and Thompson, Kenneth, W., *Principles and Problems in International Politics* (New York: Alfred A. Knopf, 1950).

Mukherjee, Sobhanlal, *International Law* (Calcutta: A Mullick and Co. 1968).

Mukherji, Sadhan, *Terrorism and Autonov Case* (Delhi: Navyug Press, 1985).

Murphy, John F., *State Support of International Terrorism: Legal, Political and Economic Dimensions* (Boulder: Westview Press, 1989).

Musa, Mohammad (Gen.), *My Version: India-Pakistan War 1965* (Lahore: Wasdalis Ltd., 1983).

Nayar, Kuldip, *Distant Neighbour: A Tale of the Sub-Continent* (Delhi: Vikas Publishing House, 1972).

Netanyahu, Benjamin (Ed.), *Terrorism: How the West Can Win?* (New York: Farrar, 1986).

Nicolson, Harold, *The Evolution of Diplomatic Method* (London: Constable & Co. 1954).

—, *Diplomacy* (London: Oxford University Press, 1963).

Norton, Augustus R. and Greenberg, Martin H., *Studies in Nuclear Terrorism* (Boston: G. K. Hall, 1979).

O'Neill, Bard E. Heaton, William, R. and Alberts, Donald J., *Insurgency in the Modern World* (Colarado: Westview Press, 1980).

Osanka, Franklin Mark, *Modern Guerilla Warfare* (New York: The Free Press of Gilencoe, 1962).

Ostrovsky, Victor and Hoy, Claire, *By Way of Deception* (London: Arrow Books, 1991).

Paget, Julien, *Counter-Insurgency Campaign* (London: Faber & Faber, 1967).

Palmer, Norman and Parkins, Howard, *International Relations* (Calcutta: Scientific Books, 1965).

Parry, Albert, *Terrorism: From Robespierre to Arafat* (New York: Vanguard Press, 1976).

Pasha, Aftab Kamal, *Libya and the US* (New Delhi: Détente Publications, 1984).

Paul, Leslie, *The Age of Terror* (Boston: The Beacon Press, 1951).

Payne, Robert, *Zero: Story of Terrorism* (New York: John Jay, 1950).

—, *The Terrorists: The Story of the Forerunners of Stalin* (New York: Funk and Wagnalls, 1957).

Radhakrishnan, S. *Indian Philosophy* (London: George Allen & Unwin, 1923).

Rosenau, James M., *A Scientific Study of Foreign Policy* (New York: The Free Press, 1971).

—, *International Politics and Foreign Policy: A Reader in Research and Theory* (New York: Free Press, 1961).

Rowan, Richard Wilmer, *Terror in Our Time* (London: Hutchinson & Co., year of publication not mentioned, acquisition in the University of Bombay Library, 1944).

Rubenstein, Richard E., *Alchemists of Revolution* (New York: Basic Books, 1987).

Russel, Bertrand, *Power: A New Analysis* (London: George Allen & Unwin, 1938).

Saksena, N. S., *Terrorism: History and Facts in the World and in India* (New Delhi: Abhinav Publications, 1985).

Sareen, Rajendra, *Pakistan: The India Factor* (New Delhi: Allied Publishers, 1984).

Scott, Andrew M. et al., *Insurgency* (Carolina: University of North

Carolina Press, 1970).

Schuman, Frederick L., *The Cold War* (Louisiana: Lousiana State University Press, 1962).

Segaller, Stephen, *Invisible Armies: Terrorism into the 1990s* (London: Michael Joseph, 1986).

Sehlagheck, D. M., *International Terrorism: An Introduction to Concepts and Actors* (Massachusetts: Lexington Books, 1988).

Selth, Andrew, *Against Every Human Law* (Sydney: Australian National University Press, 1988).

Sen, L. P., *Slender Was the Thread* (New Delhi: Sangam Books, 1973).

Sharma, Shri Ram, *Punjab in Fernent* (New Delhi: S. Chand & Co. 1971).

Siddiqi, Aslam, *Pakistan Seeks Security* (Lahore: Longman's Green & Co., 1960).

Singh, Amrik, *Punjab in Indian Politics* (Delhi: Ajanta Publications, 1985).

Singh, Gobinder, *Religion and Politics in Punjab* (New Delhi: Deep and Deep, 1986).

Singh, Gopal, *A History of Sikh People* (New Delhi: World Book Centre, 1979).

Singh, Gurmit, *History of Sikh Struggles* (New Delhi: Atlantic ublishers, 1989).

Singh, Jagjit, *The Sikh Revolution* (New Delhi: Bahri Publications, 1981).

Singh, Khushwant, *A History of Sikhs* (Delhi: Oxford University Press, 1977).

Singh, Kirpal, *The Partition of Punjab* (Patiala: Punjab University Press, 1972).

Singh, Lakshman, *Indian Swords Strike in East Pakistan* (New Delhi: Vikas Publishing, 1979).

Singh, Patwant and Malik, *Punjab: The Fatal Calculation* (New Delhi: Patwant Singh, 1985).

Singh, Satinder, *Khalistan: An Academic Analysis* (New Delhi: Amar Prakashan, 1982).

Singh, Teja and Singh, Ganda, *A Short History of the Sikhs* (New Delhi: Orient Longman, 1985).

Snyder, Richard et al., *Foreign Policy Decision Making* (New York: The Free Press, 1962).

Solzhenitsyn, Alexander, *Gulaq Archipelago* (Collins: Fontana, 1976).

Stephens, Ian, *Pakistan: Old Country New Nation* (Middlesex: Penguin Books, 1964).

Stohl, Michael, *State as Terrorists: The Dynamics of Governmental Violence and Repression* (London: Aldwin Press, 1984).

——, *The Politics of Terrorism* (New York: Marcel and Dekker, 1979).

——, *The Politics of Terror* (New York: Marcel Dekker, 1977).

Subrahmanyam, K., *Indian Security Perspectives* (New Delhi: ABC Publishing House, 1982).

Thakrah, John Richard, *Encyclopaedia of Terrorism and Political Violence* (London: Routledge and Kegan Paul, 1987).

Thapar, Romila, *A History of India* (Delhi: Penguin Books, 1966).

Thompson, David, *Europe Since Napolean* (New York: Penguin Books, 1966).

Tiwari, S.C., *Terrorism in India* (New Delhi: South Asia Publishers, 1990).

Trotsky, Leon, The Defence of Terrorism and Communism (London: George Allen & Unwin, 1935).

——, *Against Individual Terrorism* (New York: Pathfinder Press, 1974).

Turner, Admiral Stransfield, *Terrorism and Democracy* (Boston: Houghton Mifin Co., 1991).

Wallace, Paul and Chopra, Surendra, *Political Dynamics of Punjab* (Amritsar: Gurunanak Dev University, 1981).

Walzer, Michael, *Political Principles* (New York: Basic Books, 1980).

Wardlaw, Grant, *Political Terrorism: Theory, Tactics and Counter Measures* (London: Cambridge University Press, 1982).

Watson, Francis H., *Political Terrorism: The Threat and the Response* (Washington: Robert Luce Co., 1976).

Wilkinson, Paul, *Contemporary Research on Terrorism* (Aberdan: Aberdan University Press, 1987).

——, *Terrorism and the Liberal State* (New York: John Wiley and Son, 1977).

——, *Political Terrorism* (New York: John, Wiley and Sons, 1974).

Wise, David and Ross, Thomas B., *The Invisible Government* (London: Jonathan Cape, 1964).

Wolpert Stanley, *Roots of Confrontation in South Asia* (New York:

Oxford University Press, 1982).

Woodward, Bob, *Veil: The Secret War of CIA* (New York: Simon and Shuster, 1987).

Wright, Peter and Grass, Paul Green, *Spy Catcher* (New York: Viking, 1987).

Wright, Quincy, *The Role of International Law in the Elimination of War* (New York: Oceana Publications, 1961).

Ziaullah, Syed and Baid, Samuel, *Pakistan: An End Without Beginning* (New Delhi: Lancer International, 1985).

JOURNALS

Agyeman, Opoku, "Terrorism: A Non-Western View", *Monthly Review*, 39, 1987.

Alexander, Yonah, "Terrorism: The Media and The Police", *Journal of International Affairs*, 32, Spring/Summer, 1978.

—, Baum, Phil and Danziger, Raphael, "Terrorism: Future Threats and Responses", *Terrorism: An International Journal*, 4, 1985.

Arblaster, Anthony, "Terrorism: Myths, Meaning and Morals". *Political Studies*, Vol.25, No.3, 1977.

Atkinson, Scott E. et al., "Terrorism in a Bargaining Framework", *Journal of Law and Economics*, 30, 1987.

Beichman, Arnold, "A War Without End", *The American Spectator*, April, 1978.

Bell, J. Bowyer, "Transnational Terror and World Order", *South Atlantic Quarterly*, 74, Autumn, 1975.

Beres, Louis, R., "Guerrillas Terorists and Polarity: New Structural Models of World Politics", *The Western Political Quarterly*, 27, 1974.

Berry, Nicholas, O. "Theories on the Efficacy of Terrorism", *Conflict Quarterly*, 7, Winter, 1987.

Buckley, Alan O., "International terrorism", *Jounal of International Affairs*, 32, Spring/Summer, 1978.

Congressional Digest, Vol.67, No.92, (December, 1988). Crenshaw, Martha, "An Organizational Approach to the Analysis of Political Terrorism", *Orbis*, Vol.29, No.3, Fall, 1985.

—, "Theories of Terrorism", *The Journal of Strategic Studies*, Vol.10, No.4, (December, 1987).

"Economic Sanctions to Combat International Terrorism", *Department of State Bulletin*, 86, October, 1986.

Dhar, P. N., "The Kashmir Problem: Political and Economic Background", *India Quarterly*, Vol.VIII, No.62, 1951.

Dimitrivijevic, Vojin, "The Non-Aligned Movement and International Terrorism", *Review of International Affairs*, 39, March, 1987.

Elliot, John D., "Transitions of Contemporary Terrorism", *Military Review*, May, 1977.

Evans, Ailova E., "Aircraft Highjacking: What is to be done", *American Journal of International Law*, 66, 1972.

Friedlander, Robert A., "The Origins of International Terrorism: A Micro Legal Historical perspective", *Israel Year Book on Human Rights*, 6, 1976.

Fromkin, David, "The Strategy of Terrorism", *Foreign Affairs*, 53, July, 1975.

Geortz, Gary and Diehl, P.T., "Towards a Theory of International Norms", *Journal of Conflict Resolution*, Vol.36, No.4, December, 1992.

Griesman, H.C., "Social Meanings of Terrorism: Ramification, Violene and Social Control", *Contemporary Crisis*,1 July, 1977.

Guiltung, Johan, "A Structural Theory of Aggression", *Journal of Peace Research*, 2, 1964.

Horwitz, Irving L., "Political Terrorism and State Power", *Journal of Political and Military Sociology*, 1, Spring,1973.

Hutchinson, Martha Crenshaw, "Transnational Terrorism and World Politics", *Jerusalem Journal of International Realtions*, 1, Winter, 1975.

Jenkins, Brian M., "International Terrorism: Trends and Potentialities", *Journal of International Affairs*, 32, Spring/Summer, 1978.

—, "International Terrorism: A Balance Sheet", *Survival*, July/August, 1975.

Johnson, P., "The Age of Terror", *New Statesman*, 88, 1974.

Kaplan, J.J., "The United States Foreign Aid Programme: Past Perspectives and Future Needs", *World Politics*, Vol. 3, October, 1950.

Kaul, T.N., "Kashmir: What is at Stake?" *World Affairs*, Vol.1, No.2, December, 1992.

Kennedy, Mooreheads, "The Root Cause of Terrorism: Terrorism and Retribution will be a self-perpetuating phenomenon unless we seek to understand its sources", *Humanist*, 46, September/October, 1986.

Kissinger, Henry A., "Highjacking, Terrorism and War", *Department of State Bulletin*, 73, September, 1975.

Lacqueur, Walter, "Reflections on Terrorism", *Foreign Affairs*, 65, Fall, 1986.

Legun, Colin, "The Rise of Terrorism", *Current*, 147, January, 1973.

Lewis, William H. and Joyner, Christopher C., "Quaddafi is Brewing up Trouble for Bush", *New York Times*, December, 1988.

Lowenthal, Abraham F., "Foreign Aid as a Political Instrument: A Case S tudy of the Dominican Republic, 1961-63", *Public Policy*, Vol.XIV, 1965.

Marwah, Ved, "Role of Terrorism in Foreign Policy", *Times of India* (New Dehi), 23rd July, 1992.

May, W. F., "Terrorism as Strategy and Ecstasy", *Social Research*, 41, Summer, 1974.

Metz, Steven, "The Ideology of Terrorist Foreign Policy in Libya and South Africa", *Conflict: An International Journal*, Vol.7, No.4, 1987.

Mickolus, Edward F., "Chronology of Transnational Terrorist Attacks Upon American Business People", *Terrorism: An International Journal*, 1, 1978.

Miller, Reuben, "Acts of International Terrorism: Government Response and Policies", *Comparative Political Studies*, 19, October, 1986.

Neale, William D., "Terror: Oldest Weapon in the Arsenal", *Army*, August, 1973.

O'Brien, Conor Cruise. "Liberty and Terror", *Encounter*, October, 1977.

—, "On Violence and Terror", *Dissent*, 24, Fall, 1977.

—, "Liberty and Terrorism", *International Security*, 2, Fall, 1977.

Peterson, R.W., "International Terrorism Threat Analysis", *National Technical Information Service* (S.), 1977.

Pierre, Andrew J., "The Politics of International Terrorism", *Orbis*, 19, Winter, 1976.

Quinterre Morente, Frederico, "Terrorism", *Military Review*, December, 1965.

Rizvi, Hasan Askari, "Pakistan: Ideology and Foreign Policy", *Asian Affairs*, Spring, 1983.

Robertson, K.G., "Intelligence , Terrorism and Civil Liberties", *Conflict Quarterly*, 7, Spring, 1987.

Rose, Leo E., "Pakistan Role and Interests in South and South West Asia", *Asian Affairs*, 9, September/October, 1981.

Russell, Charles A., "Transnational Terrorism", *Air University Review*, Vol.XXVII, No.2, January/February, 1976.

—, and Miller, Bowman H., "Profiles of a Terrorist", *Military Review*, August, 1977.

Salter, Leonard M., "Terrorism: Towards an International Criminal Court", *The Law Magazine*, November, 1987.

Serge, D.U. and Adler, J.H., "Ecology of Terrorism", *Encounter*, 40, February, 1973.

Shultz, Richard Jr., "Can Democratic Governments Use Military Force in the War Against Terrorism?", *World Affairs*, 148, Spring, 1986.

—, "Conceptualizing Political Terrorism: A Typology", *Journal Of International Affairs*, 32, Spring/Summer, 1978.

Silverman, Jerry M. and Jackson, Peter M., "Terror in Insurgency Warfare", *Military Review*, October, 1970.

Simon, Jeffrey O., "Misunderstanding Terrorism", *Foreign Policy*, No.67, Summer, 1987.

Sloan, Stephen and Kearney, Richard, "Non-territorial Terrorism: An Empirical Approach to Policy Formation", *Conflict: An International Journal for Conflict and Policy*, 1978.

Smart, Ian M. H., "The Power of Terror", *International Journal*, Vol.30, Spring, 1975.

Sofaer, D. Abraham, "Terrorism and the Law", *Foreign Affairs*, Vol.64/5, 1986.

St. John Ronald Bruce, "Terrorism and Libyan Foreign Policy – 1981-1986", *World Today*, 42, July, 1986.

Subrawardy, H.S., "Political Stability and Democracy in Pakistan", *Foreign Affairs*, Vol. 35, No.1-4, April, 1957.

Wapner, Paul, "Problems of U.S. Counter-terrorism: The Case of Libya", *Alternatives*, Vol.XII, No.2, April, 1988.

Wilkinson, Paul, "Can the State be Terorist?", *International Affairs*, Vol.57, No.3, Summer, 1981.

Wolf, John B., "Terrorist Manipulation of The Democratic Process", *Police Journal*, 48, April/June, 1975.

Wolfgang, Marvin E., (Special Editor), "International Terrorism",

(Special Number), *Annals of the American Academy of Political Science*, Vol.436, September, 1982.

NEWSPAPERS AND MAGAZINES

The Business and Political Weekly (Bombay) 29th November, 1991.

The Daily (Bombay) 9th November, 1992.

Deccan Herald (Bangalore) 9th November, 1992.

The Economic Times (Bombay) 21st July, 1992.

The Hindu (Madras) 13th August, 1992.

Illustrated Weekly of India (Bombay) 2nd June, 1985.

India Today (Delhi) 31st October, 1991.

— 15th July, 1992.

— 31st December, 1992.

— 15th December, 1993.

Indian Express (Bombay) 5th May, 1991.

— 5th October, 1991.

— 29th October, 1991.

— 18th December, 1991.

— 29th February, 1992.

— 1st March, 1992.

— 23rd March, 1992.

— 12th June, 1992.

— 18th July, 1992.

— 25th April, 1993.

— 10th July, 1993.

— 31st August, 1993.

The Observer (New Delhi), 8th October, 1992.

The Pioneer (New Delhi) 31st January, 1993.

The Statesman (New Delhi) 1st October, 1992.

— (Calcutta), 7th July, 1946

Sunday (Calcutta) 24th March, 1991.

— 26th April - 2nd May, 1992.

Sunday Observer (Bombay) 7th June, 1992.

— 27th November, 1994.

Surya India (New Delhi) 16th December, 1983.

Times of India (Bombay) 15th December, 1991.

— 12th January, 1992.

— 6th March, 1992.

— 23rd July, 1992.

— 31st August, 1992.

The Telegraph (Calcutta) 2nd December, 1983.

— 31st December, 1992.

— 8th January, 1993.

The Tribune (Ambala) 19th July, 1959.

— (Chandigarh) 12th March, 1987.

The Week (Bombay) 8th September, 1991.

Index